CAMPAIGN 428

GRENADA 1983

American Resurgence Toward the End of the Cold War

MATTHEW A. FRAKES   ILLUSTRATED BY JOHNNY SHUMATE

OSPREY PUBLISHING
Bloomsbury Publishing Plc
Kemp House, Chawley Park, Cumnor Hill, Oxford OX2 9PH, UK
Bloomsbury Publishing Ireland Limited,
29 Earlsfort Terrace, Dublin 2, D02 AY28, Ireland
Bloomsbury Publishing Inc.
1359 Broadway, 12th Floor, New York, NY 10018, USA
E-mail: info@ospreypublishing.com
www.ospreypublishing.com

OSPREY is a trademark of Osprey Publishing Ltd

First published in Great Britain in 2026

A catalog record for this book is available from the British Library.

ISBN: PB 9781472868497; eBook 9781472868503; ePDF 9781472868527;
XML 9781472868510

26 27 28 29 30 10 9 8 7 6 5 4 3 2 1

Maps by Bounford.com
3D BEV by Paul Kime
Index by Fionbar Lyons
Typeset by Lumina Datamatics Ltd
Printed by Repro India Ltd

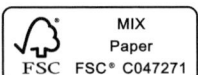

Osprey Publishing supports the Woodland Trust, the UK's leading woodland
conservation charity.

To find out more about our authors and books visit
www.ospreypublishing.com. Here you will find extracts, author
interviews, details of forthcoming events and the option to sign up for
our newsletter.

For product safety related questions contact
productsafety@bloomsbury.com

Key to military symbols

Army Group	Army	Corps	Division	Brigade	Regiment	Battalion
Company/Battery	Platoon	Section	Squad	Infantry	Artillery	Cavalry
Airborne	Unit HQ	Air defense	Air Force	Air mobile	Air transportable	Amphibious
Antitank	Armor	Air aviation	Bridging	Engineer	Headquarters	Maintenance
Medical	Missile	Mountain	Navy	Nuclear, biological, chemical	Ordnance	Parachute
Reconnaissance	Signal	Supply	Transport movement	Rocket artillery	Air defense artillery	

Key to unit identification

Unit identifier — Parent unit — Commander
(+) with added elements
(−) less elements

Front cover main illustration: Rangers' parachute assault on Point Salines
Airport, 0552hrs, October 25, 1983. (Johnny Shumate)
Title page photograph: Vice Adm. Joseph Metcalf speaks with a group of
Army Rangers before the mission to rescue medical students from the
Grand Anse medical school campus. (National Archives)

CONTENTS

Strategic view of Grenada and the Caribbean, 1983

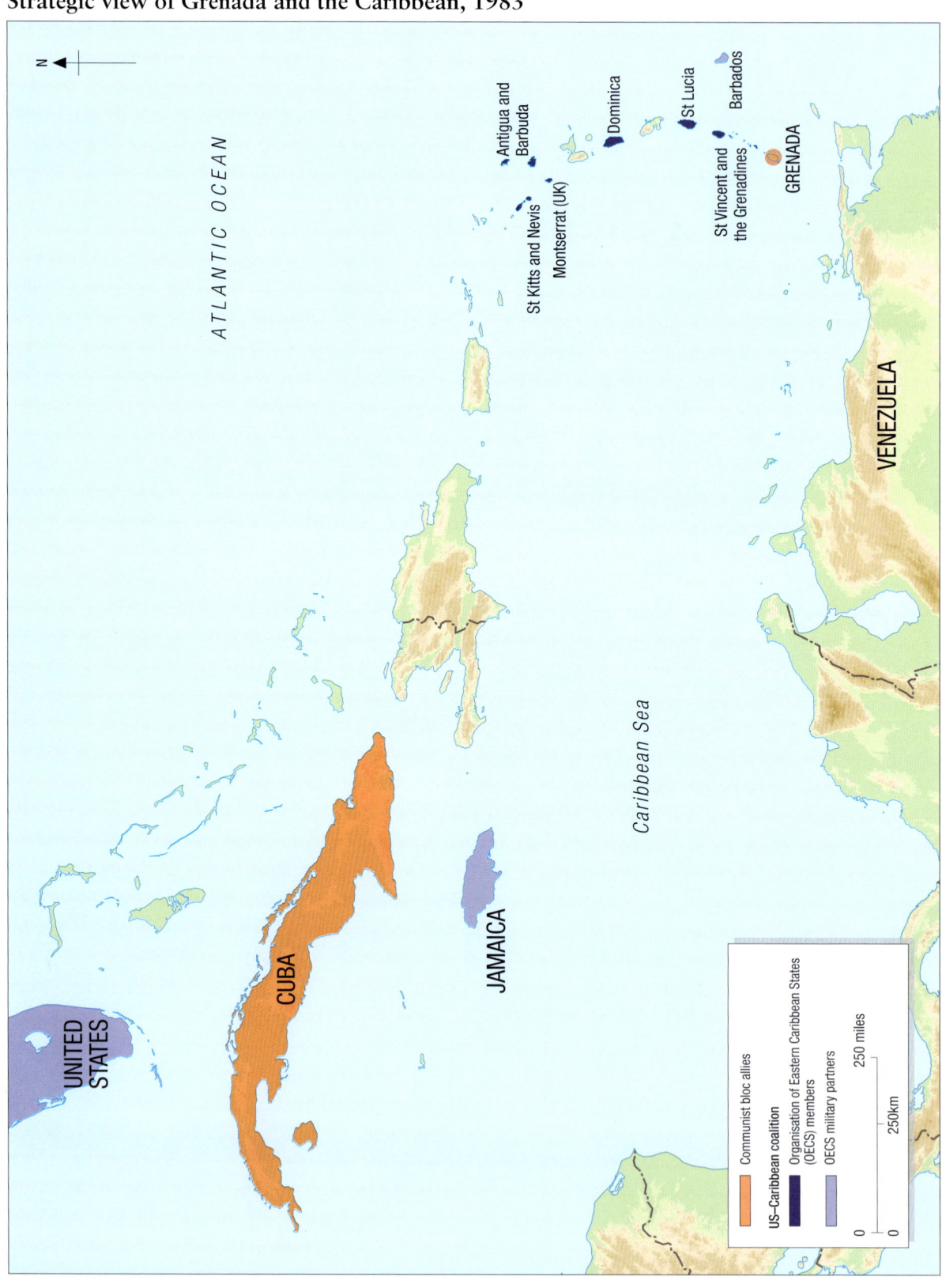

N

ATLANTIC OCEAN

Antigua and
Barbuda

Dominica

St Lucia

Barbados

St Kitts and Nevis

Montserrat (UK)

St Vincent and
the Grenadines

GRENADA

VENEZUELA

Caribbean Sea

CUBA

JAMAICA

UNITED
STATES

Communist bloc allies

US-Caribbean coalition

Organisation of Eastern Caribbean States
(OECS) members

OECS military partners

250 miles

250km

0

0

ORIGINS OF THE CAMPAIGN

"We got there just in time." Speaking from the Oval Office, President Ronald Reagan explained to the nation why he had sent American military forces into combat on the tiny Caribbean island of Grenada in late October 1983. Reagan noted that the island was only twice the size of the District of Columbia, and most Americans would have been hard-pressed to find it on a map just a few days earlier. Yet for two weeks in the fall of 1983, this small island took center stage in the world's attention, as a local political power struggle escalated into a regional conflict involving the military might of a Cold War superpower with consequences that would reverberate around the globe.

The American invasion of Grenada in October 1983 was the largest and most significant US military operation since the end of the Vietnam War a decade earlier. This was the only time that President Reagan deployed American ground forces in combat during his presidency. The campaign showcased growing US military effectiveness and morale following Reagan's expansion and modernization of the armed forces. The successes and flaws in the execution of this joint-forces operation led to reforms that decisively shaped the US military for the end of the Cold War and the conflicts of the post-Cold War world.

The Grenada campaign fell at the most dangerous moment in the Cold War since the Cuban Missile Crisis almost exactly 21 years earlier. The broader global context of the Cold War is critical to understanding why a local political crisis so rapidly ballooned into a military conflict with far-reaching international implications. Reagan had entered office in January 1981 determined to revive America's capacity and resolve to wage and win the Cold War struggle against Soviet communism. He combined the largest peacetime military buildup in US history with tough rhetoric against the Soviet Union, which he condemned as the "evil empire" in March 1983. By the fall of 1983, tensions between the United States and the Soviet Union had escalated to the point of crisis when Soviet military forces shot down a Korean civilian airliner that had veered into Soviet airspace, killing all

In a nationally televised address from the Oval Office in March 1983, US President Ronald Reagan warned of the "Soviet–Cuban militarization of Grenada" that was "unrelated to any conceivable threat to this island country" and displayed surveillance photographs of the military-grade airport under construction at Point Salines. (Courtesy Ronald Reagan Presidential Library)

Grenadian leader Maurice Bishop forged close ties with Cuba's Fidel Castro, with whom he is shown in July 1983. Bishop sought Cuba's aid in vastly expanding Grenada's military capabilities, but his grand plans remained mostly unfulfilled in October 1983. (Bettmann/Getty Images)

Bernard Coard served as Bishop's deputy prime minister prior to ousting him in a coup. Longtime friends and rivals, the two were opposites in style and temperament: Bishop the charismatic populist, Coard the organizational technocrat and ideological leader of the socialist party. (US Department of Defense)

269 on board, including 62 Americans. In November, the US was scheduled to stage military exercises with its NATO allies to simulate a nuclear war with the Soviet Union. That same month, the US would also begin deploying a new class of nuclear weapons in Western Europe, prompting anxieties from civilians and Soviet officials alike that the Cold War was on the verge of turning hot.

Into this cauldron came an internal power struggle on the island of Grenada. Standing at the southernmost end of the Windward island chain of the Lesser Antilles, just north of Venezuela, Grenada guards the strategically valuable shipping lanes between the Caribbean Sea and the Atlantic Ocean. Once part of the British Empire, Grenada had gained its independence in 1974 but remained part of the Commonwealth, with Queen Elizabeth II as head of state, represented by a local governor-general. Its population of 90,000 in 1983 had dropped by 10,000 in the four years of political repression and economic decline since 1979 as many Grenadians fled overseas. It was in March 1979 that Grenada first seized the attention of policymakers in the halls of Washington, when a group of Marxists staged a nearly bloodless coup to oust the island's autocratic and unpopular prime minister and suspend the 1974 democratic constitution, establishing in its place a socialist regime called the People's Revolutionary Government (PRG). Maurice Bishop, the charismatic leader of the socialist political party called the New Jewel Movement (NJM), seized control of the country as prime minister and initially enjoyed wide support from the Grenadian people.

After he seized power in 1979, Bishop fashioned grand plans for the militarization of his island nation. He quickly signed military aid agreements with Cuba and the Soviet Union, both of which sent military instructors and vast shipments of weapons. This military buildup on Grenada sparked fears and suspicions in Washington that Cuba and the Soviet Union were transforming the island, as Reagan would later explain, into "a major military bastion to export terror and undermine democracy" by spreading communist revolution throughout the region. In particular, Reagan pointed to Bishop's plans to construct a new airport at Point Salines with a 10,000ft runway, which was nearing completion by the fall of 1983, with Cuban funding and construction aid. This project was ostensibly for civilian purposes but was also capable of supporting long-range military aircraft.

Ironically, it was the murder of this close partner of Fidel Castro and growing ally of the Soviet Union that precipitated American military intervention on Grenada. Little known to the Americans, a power struggle was gathering steam within the leadership ranks of the NJM and the PRG. As the Grenadian economy increasingly faltered and the socialist revolution veered toward collapse, opposition to Bishop's leadership coalesced around the deputy prime minister, Bernard Coard, who championed a hardline Marxist–Leninist stance as the solution to Grenada's woes.

The immediate crisis on Grenada that would culminate in the US-led invasion began on October 12–13, when the power struggle within the PRG spilled over into the public arena as Bishop pushed to maintain his hold on power. Coard's doctrinaire Marxist–Leninist faction, which held the loyalty of most of the Grenadian army's officer corps, responded to Bishop's defiance by placing him under house arrest. The shocking news of Bishop's ousting as prime minister sparked public demonstrations across the island of such magnitude that Coard decided to resign and wield power instead from behind the scenes, but this move did little to quell the public's outrage against his faction's power grab.

The tipping point of the leadership crisis on Grenada came on October 19, which Grenadians would know ever after as "Bloody Wednesday." That morning, a crowd of about 5,000 pro-Bishop protestors marched to the prime minister's residence to free him from house arrest, then followed him to the military headquarters at Fort Rupert in the capital city, St George's, which he occupied without a struggle. Coard and his allies, meeting at another military command post at Fort Frederick, ordered armored units of the People's Revolutionary Army (PRA) to attack and recapture Fort Rupert. After a bloody exchange of fire, the PRA attackers captured Bishop and then sought guidance from Coard and his deputies, who ordered that Bishop be executed immediately. The PRA soldiers formed a firing squad and summarily shot Bishop, alongside seven of his chief supporters, in an inner courtyard of Fort Rupert.

In the aftermath of Bishop's execution, the clique at Fort Frederick agreed to form an interim government called the Revolutionary Military Council (RMC), composed of 16 PRA officers who were loyal to Coard. The official public leader of the RMC was Gen. Hudson Austin, the minister of defense under Bishop and commander of the PRA, whose prominent role in the 1979 revolution that had brought Bishop to power lent public credibility to the new regime. But behind the scenes Coard was the true leader, wielding power and directing policy for the RMC while trying to keep a low public profile. That night, Austin announced a 24-hour "shoot-on-sight" curfew in an ill-fated attempt to maintain public order, an act that only magnified the violent and extremist nature of the new regime in the eyes of the Grenadian people, Grenada's Caribbean neighbors, and the United States.

Officials in the Reagan administration viewed the chaos on Grenada as a communist power projection into the Caribbean and the Western Hemisphere. They assumed that the hardline Marxist coup led by Coard could not have happened without the approval and even instigation of Cuba or the Soviet Union. Though mistaken, this perception hardened their resolve to take action. As Reagan's national security advisor, Robert McFarlane, later wrote, "The prospect of a second Cuba at our doorstep, with all that implied for the export of revolution to countries in South America, was a serious challenge from Moscow. We were going to have to act."

Civilians flee from PRA armored vehicles during the "Bloody Wednesday" attack on Fort Rupert, October 19, 1983. PRA soldiers fired into the crowd of protestors supporting Bishop, killing at least eight civilians and wounding another hundred. (US Department of Defense)

Grenada, 1983

N

Caribbean Sea

Carriacou
(18 miles)

Sauteurs

Victoria

Gouyave

Mount St Catherine

Pearls
Airport

Grenville

BEAUSÉJOUR BAY   Beauséjour

**Radio Free Grenada
Transmitter Station**

GRAND MAL BAY

St George's   Mount Wheldale (Government House)

Fort Rupert

Fort Frederick

**Richmond Hill
Prison**

St George's Harbour

Grand Anse
Beach

**Grand Anse Medical
School Campus**

Frequente

Calliste

Amber
Belair

**Calivigny
Military Compound**

Westerhall Point

ATLANTIC OCEAN

Point Salines
Airport

**True Blue
Medical School
Campus**

Lance aux Épines

0		3 miles

0	3km	

CHRONOLOGY

1974

February 7   Grenada gains independence from Britain.

1976

July 23   American investors found St George's University School of Medicine on Grenada.

1979

March 13   Maurice Bishop seizes power in a coup and establishes a socialist government on Grenada, fostering close ties with Cuba.

November 17   Bishop announces plans to construct a new airport at Point Salines with Cuban aid.

1980

October 27   Grenada signs a secret military aid agreement with the Soviet Union.

1983

March 23   In an Oval Office address, Ronald Reagan warns of the "Soviet–Cuban militarization of Grenada" and the construction of a new military-grade airport.

October 12–13   Bishop is placed under house arrest following a power struggle within the Grenadian government.

October 19   "Bloody Wednesday": Bishop is freed but recaptured and executed by the Grenadian military; the Revolutionary Military Council (RMC) is formed as an interim government and imposes a shoot-on-sight curfew.

October 21   The Organisation of Eastern Caribbean States (OECS) unanimously decides to intervene in Grenada and request military assistance from the US, Britain, Jamaica, and Barbados.

October 22   Reagan gives preliminary approval to the OECS request for US military intervention to restore order and democracy to Grenada.

October 23   Terrorists bomb the US Marine barracks in Beirut, Lebanon; Reagan signs the official order to execute the military operation on Grenada; Joint Task Force 120 is activated with Vice Adm. Joseph Metcalf in command; Navy SEALs abort reconnaissance of Point Salines Airport.

October 24   US commanders finalize plans for the invasion; Cuban Col. Pedro Tortoló Comas arrives on Grenada to organize Cuban defenses; Reagan gives final approval to execute the operation; Navy SEALs abort a second reconnaissance of Point Salines Airport but scout the beach near Pearls Airport.

October 25   Operation *Urgent Fury* begins: Marines capture Pearls Airport and Grenville; Rangers secure Point Salines Airport and the True Blue medical school campus; special operations forces face heavy Grenadian resistance around St George's; Marines make an amphibious landing north of St George's.

October 26	Grenada's military leadership goes into hiding as organized Grenadian resistance crumbles; US forces bring Grenada's governor-general to safety, capture the Cuban headquarters compound, and rescue medical students at the Grand Anse campus.
October 27	Marines advance into St George's; Rangers assault the PRA compound at Calivigny; Reagan delivers an Oval Office address on the crisis.
October 28	Army and Marine forces link up south of St George's and secure more American students.
November 1	Marines land on Carriacou, encountering no resistance.
November 2	US commanders declare an official end of hostilities.
November 15	Governor-General Paul Scoon appoints an interim government to organize new elections on Grenada.
December 12	The last US combat forces leave Grenada.

1984

December 3	Grenada holds democratic elections.

1986

February 20	Reagan visits Grenada.
October 1	Reagan signs the Goldwater–Nichols Act, reforming the US military with lessons from Grenada.
December 4	RMC leaders are convicted of murdering Bishop.

US Army Rangers, shown here landing in Marine helicopters on Grand Anse Beach to rescue American medical students on October 26, shouldered the heaviest burden of fighting on Grenada. In both its successes and failures, the Grenada campaign became a model for conducting short-notice contingency missions that brought together units from all branches of the US military. (Mike Leahy, Navy Art Collection, Naval History and Heritage Command)

OPPOSING COMMANDERS

UNITED STATES

Vice Admiral Joseph Metcalf III (1927–2007) served as the overall commander of US forces conducting Operation *Urgent Fury*, the largest US military combat operation since the end of the Vietnam War. He enlisted in the US Navy at age 19 before graduating from the Naval Academy at Annapolis, and he subsequently held sea commands as well as staff assignments at each rank from lieutenant to vice admiral. His experience commanding the Navy surface ships involved in the 1975 evacuation of US forces from Saigon in South Vietnam prepared him to lead a rescue mission in which the evacuation of US nationals was a key part. Three months prior to the Grenada operation, Metcalf took command of the US Second Fleet, with responsibility for the western Atlantic. Metcalf did not learn that he would command the Grenada operation until October 23, 1983, and played no role in the initial planning. Given only 39 hours to prepare, Metcalf arrived on his flagship, USS *Guam*, on the evening of October 24, just hours before the invasion began. Following the Grenada operation, Metcalf became the deputy chief of staff of naval operations for surface warfare before retiring from active service in 1987.

Major General H. Norman Schwarzkopf (1934–2012) held two key posts during Operation *Urgent Fury*: first as the chief US Army advisor assigned to Vice Adm. Metcalf's staff aboard USS *Guam* and then as Metcalf's deputy commander for Joint Task Force 120. By 1983, when he commanded the 24th Mechanized Infantry Division as a two-star general, Schwarzkopf had earned a reputation as a tough, battle-tested combat commander who graduated from West Point and served two highly decorated tours of duty in Vietnam, for which he was awarded two Purple Hearts and three Silver Stars for bravery. Schwarzkopf received the unexpected order to serve

The two top American commanders in Grenada formed an effective team: Navy Vice Adm. Joseph Metcalf compensated for his limited knowledge of ground warfare by developing a close working relationship with his Army advisor and later deputy commander, Maj. Gen. Norman Schwarzkopf, whose influence proved decisive at several critical moments in the campaign. (US Department of Defense)

as Metcalf's Army advisor, outside the chain of command, on October 23, and Metcalf formally made Schwarzkopf his deputy commander – and therefore the single overall ground force commander – on the evening of October 26. Schwarzkopf later rose to the rank of four-star general and served as commander of US Central Command, where he led US and coalition forces to victory over Iraq in Operations *Desert Shield* and *Desert Storm* of the Gulf War in 1990–91.

Major General Richard Scholtes (1934–) commanded the special operations forces that carried out the attack on Point Salines Airport and the missions around St George's on the first day of the Grenada operation. An experienced soldier who enlisted in the Army at age 17 before graduating from West Point, Scholtes fought in the Vietnam War and served as the first commander of the Joint Special Operations Command (JSOC). Involved in planning the Grenada operation at an early stage, Scholtes was the ranking commander of US ground forces for the most critical and most heavily contested missions on the first day of the invasion. He retired from active service in 1986

Maj. Gen. Richard Scholtes played an instrumental role in creating the Joint Special Operations Command (JSOC) in the wake of the failed Iranian hostage rescue mission in 1980. The Grenada campaign would mark JSOC's first major combat test. (National Archives)

and played an important role in the military reforms later in the decade that drew on lessons from Grenada.

Major General Edward Trobaugh (1932–2024), a graduate of West Point who had served two combat tours in the Vietnam War, commanded the 82nd Airborne Division during the Grenada operation. He was the senior commander of US ground forces on the island from his arrival on the late afternoon of October 25 until the formal end of hostilities on

Maj. Gen. Edward Trobaugh, shown here on Grenada with Joint Chiefs of Staff Chairman Gen. John Vessey, had taken command of the 82nd Airborne Division in June 1983. Experienced as an infantry leader and logistics organizer, his methodical advance from Point Salines drew criticism for its slowness in securing the full island. (National Archives)

November 2, when he assumed overall command of all US forces on Grenada from Metcalf. Following his departure from Grenada on November 9, Trobaugh remained in command of the 82nd Airborne until 1985, retiring from active service two years later.

GRENADA

General Hudson Austin (1938–2022) served as the overall commander of Grenada's military forces and chairman of the RMC, the figurehead leader of the interim regime that replaced Maurice Bishop's government on October 19, 1983. Poorly educated and with little military training, Austin was employed as a prison guard in the 1960s, where he met Bishop and rallied to his revolutionary cause. He earned a hero's reputation within Bishop's NJM for leading the military side of the 1979 coup that brought Bishop to power, and he then served as minister of defense and interior, minister of communications and construction, and commander of the People's Revolutionary Armed Forces. In these roles, he held responsibility for overseeing Grenada's army, militia, police, and security services, as well as the construction of the new military-grade airport at Point Salines. US forces captured Austin on October 30 as he sought to escape the island. He was subsequently imprisoned and convicted in 1986 for his part in Bishop's murder and sentenced to hang, but his death sentence was later commuted to life in prison and he was released in 2008.

Gen. Hudson Austin was the public leader of the new regime that deposed Bishop, but Coard pulled the strings of power behind the scenes. Likewise, Austin's involvement in military decision-making after the invasion began was minimal, deferring instead to his military subordinates. (US Department of Defense)

CUBA

Colonel Pedro Tortoló Comas (1945–), a career military officer who was then serving in the prominent post of chief of staff of the Army of the Center, was chosen by Cuban leader Fidel Castro to command Cuban forces on Grenada for both his military experience and his firsthand knowledge of Grenada and its leaders. Until May 1983, Tortoló had served as the chief of the Cuban military mission to Grenada, overseeing the influx of military advisors and equipment that followed the 1979 socialist coup under Maurice Bishop. Tortoló returned to Grenada on October 24, the day before the invasion began, to take charge of organizing the defense of the Cuban camps near Point Salines Airport. The poor performance of Cuban forces during the campaign led to his disgrace upon his return to Cuba, where he was court-martialed and demoted to private in a ceremony in which Defense Minister Raúl Castro ripped his rank insignia from the shoulders of his uniform. He then faded into obscurity and later resurfaced as a taxi driver in Havana.

OPPOSING FORCES

UNITED STATES

The United States mission on Grenada brought together units and commanders from every branch of the armed services. Joint Task Force 120, under the command of Vice Adm. Joseph Metcalf, was the umbrella for all US forces that would take part in the Grenada invasion. The organization and command structure of Joint Task Force 120 consisted of four essential parts, each designated as a separate task force with a commander who reported to Metcalf: the special forces, an amphibious force of naval and Marine units, the 82nd Airborne Division, and a Navy carrier battle group.

Task Force 123 included special forces units from the newly created JSOC of Maj. Gen. Richard Scholtes. Two battalions of Army Rangers from the 75th Infantry, approximately 700 strong in total, were the spearhead of the invasion. Scholtes's command also included commandos from Navy SEAL Team 6 and the Army's Delta Force, lightly armed and equipped with carbine rifles and pistols suited for stealthy nighttime insertion and extraction at key targets. Carrying them into battle were UH-60 Black Hawk helicopters from the Army's secret and newly created 160th Aviation Battalion, dubbed the "Night Stalkers" for their special training in nighttime flying.

The Rangers were an elite light infantry unit trained to make airborne landings and seize and secure airports, training that made them the ideal force for their assigned mission at Point Salines. The post-Vietnam incarnation of the Rangers had been activated in 1974, and Grenada would be their first combat test. (National Archives)

The helicopter carrier USS *Guam* served as the flagship for Joint Task Force 120 commander Vice Adm. Metcalf. The ship helped launch the Marine attack on Pearls Airport early on the operation's first day before relocating to the scene of the heaviest fighting on the island's west coast. (National Archives)

The other main ground force at the start of the invasion was the 22nd Marine Amphibious Unit (MAU) in Amphibious Squadron 4, designated Task Force 124. Aboard the squadron's five vessels were the 822 Marines of Battalion Landing Team 2/8, a six-man contingent from Navy SEAL Team 4, and support from M60A1 tanks, LVTP-7 amphibious armored personnel carriers, and the transport and attack helicopters of Marine Medium Helicopter Squadron 261 (HMM-261).

Task Force 121, comprising units from the Army's 82nd Airborne Division under Maj. Gen. Edward Trobaugh, was intended to be the follow-on occupation force. The initial units to arrive on Grenada were two battalions of the 325th Infantry, and four more battalions from the 505th and 508th Infantry eventually landed as reinforcements, each consisting of approximately 730 paratroopers.

Providing naval and air support from offshore was Task Group 20.5, formed from the six-vessel naval battle group centered on the aircraft carrier USS *Independence*. The Air Force's Military Airlift Command (MAC) supported Joint Task Force 120 by airlifting troops and supplies from bases in the US and Barbados while providing air support with AC-130 Spectre gunships.

CARIBBEAN COALITION

Military intervention on Grenada was a Caribbean-driven initiative. While the US government had grown increasingly concerned over the militarization of Grenada throughout 1983, it was Grenada's Caribbean neighbors who were the driving force behind enlisting American support for a military operation to restore order and democracy to Grenada.

The Caribbean coalition included three partners that quickly formed the Caribbean Peacekeeping Force: the Organisation of Eastern Caribbean States (OECS), Barbados, and Jamaica. The bulk of this force, which totaled 353 soldiers and policemen, came from the Jamaica Defence Force (a full rifle company of 152 soldiers from the Jamaica Regiment) and the Barbados Defence Force (a reinforced rifle platoon of 60 soldiers as well as 50 policemen from the Royal Barbados Police). The contributions from five

The Caribbean Peacekeeping Force included military units and paramilitary police forces that wore combat uniforms with helmets or berets and had military training and weapons. Most of the police forces involved wore their dress uniforms with bright colors and distinctive hats that made them stand out among the invading forces. (National Archives)

OECS member states were more modest, but only because most of these nations did not have permanent military forces. Antigua and Barbuda sent an infantry squad of 14 soldiers, while Dominica, St Lucia, and St Vincent and the Grenadines each sent a contingent of 15–20 policemen. St Kitts and Nevis, independent from Britain for only a month, sent five policemen, while Montserrat, still a British territory, was prohibited from participating in the operation by the Foreign Office in London. Morale among the Caribbean forces was high and enthusiasm for the mission strong, as policemen and constables volunteered to take up arms to end the violence on Grenada.

The Caribbean forces arrived on Grenada without a clear idea of what their role in the mission would be. As increasing numbers of Grenadian and especially Cuban forces surrendered, the Caribbean Peacekeeping Force was assigned to the non-combat role of guarding the growing number of prisoners. Once hostilities ended, Caribbean forces took over primary responsibility for the island's security following the return of American units to the United States.

Brigadier Rudyard Lewis, the chief of staff of the Barbados Defence Force, was named overall commander of the Caribbean Peacekeeping Force. Because Barbados and Jamaica had the only two standing military forces in the region that could counter the Grenadian armed forces, the two top command positions were given to these nations. (National Archives)

GRENADA

Contrary to what American commanders expected, the stoutest and most destructive resistance that the invading US forces faced came not from the Cubans but from the Grenadian military forces. The People's Revolutionary Armed Forces consisted of two military wings: the PRA and the People's Revolutionary Militia (PRM).

On paper, the PRA, Grenada's professional military force, had a total strength of 906, but barely half that number – 463 regular soldiers – answered the call to mobilize by the outbreak of fighting on October 25. Grenada had no tanks, no air force, and no navy other than a coast guard of four converted fishing vessels. The PRA was a light infantry force with the strength of one battalion, consisting of three companies plus several security platoons and an antiaircraft battery. The two strongest companies, the Motorised Company and the Mobile Company, were placed under the command of the 23-year-old Lt Raeburn Nelson as a single infantry battle group that became the PRA's main strike force. The elite Motorised Company was equipped with seven Soviet-designed BTR-60 armored personnel carriers (APCs) and two BRDM-2 armored amphibious scout cars, while the Mobile Company was equipped with trucks for rapid deployment. The third company, under the command of Lt Callistus Bernard (also known as Iman Abdullah), was the Exploration Company, a rapid mobilization company meant for reconnaissance that usually consisted of a mix of regulars and militiamen. On the eve of battle, however, its PRA personnel were transferred to other units, so it contained only militiamen. The last PRA units included security platoons, with a mix of regulars and militia under Capt. Lester Redhead, and an antiaircraft battery under the command of chief of artillery Lt Cecil Prime, equipped with six Soviet ZU 23mm antiaircraft guns and eight older Cuban 12.7mm guns.

PRA regular soldiers, shown here as prisoners, received limited training from the Cuban military advisors stationed on Grenada, who focused more on political and ideological indoctrination in the classroom than practical combat lessons in the field. (National Archives)

Most PRA soldiers were equipped with Cuban- and Soviet-supplied AK-47 automatic rifles and wore Cuban-style olive-drab uniforms with Soviet-designed helmets. The PRA officer corps was small and youthful, drawn mainly from the young men who had taken up arms with Bishop to seize power in 1979. Neither the officers nor their soldiers had any actual experience of combat outside the one-day (and nearly bloodless) coup in 1979.

The PRM was a far less reliable force, and only 257 militiamen answered the call to mobilize on the eve of the invasion – just one in ten of the nominal total strength of approximately 2,500. While the PRM officially consisted of five battalions, the militia turnout was so low that it was largely incorporated into existing PRA units rather than functioning as separate cohesive battalions during the invasion. Militiamen received minimal military training and were equipped haphazardly if at all, typically dressed in civilian clothing.

As an invasion loomed in the aftermath of the bloody coup that left Bishop dead and the Grenadian populace in shock, morale in the ranks was low, since much of the PRA and especially the PRM had been loyal to the popular and now-murdered Bishop.

CUBA

During the planning for Operation *Urgent Fury*, American policymakers and military commanders expected that their primary adversary on Grenada would be Cuba. In fact, Cuban forces on Grenada would play a limited, though not negligible, role in the fighting and would mount a far less substantial resistance than Grenadian military units, the result of the ad hoc and ill-prepared state of Cuba's personnel on the island.

The main group of Cubans on Grenada were the 636 construction workers who had been sent to carry out the work of building the new airport at Point Salines. While not active-duty professional soldiers in Cuba's Revolutionary Armed Forces, they were all military reservists and, like all Cuban citizens, had previously received military training and served in the Cuban armed forces. Supplementing their AK-47 automatic rifles were several mortars, machine guns, and recoilless rifles from the PRA supply depot. The Cubans did not have any armored vehicles or antiaircraft guns, though PRA soldiers manned several antiaircraft guns nearby. The workers were based in two military-style camps to the north of Point Salines, the "Old Camp" just north of the airport terminal and the Cuban headquarters compound near the village of Calliste, which the Americans called "Little Havana." Neither of these camps was located on a site well-situated for defense, with hills and ridges surrounding them on virtually all sides.

Leading and organizing the construction workers into military companies were the 43 military advisors stationed on Grenada to train and advise the Grenadian armed forces. These advisors were professional soldiers of all ranks, though most were technical advisors and translators rather than infantry commanders. The Cuban commander, Col. Pedro Tortoló Comas, recalled all of these military advisors from the Grenadian army to command the companies of construction workers, which would operate independently from Grenadian forces.

Most Cuban forces on Grenada were construction workers who wore civilian clothing, typically blue shirts and straw hats. Their average age was 38, with some over 50. They had never trained as a cohesive combat unit, and their motivation to mount a substantial defense was low – factors that severely limited their effectiveness. (National Archives)

ORDERS OF BATTLE

UNITED STATES AND CARIBBEAN COALITION

Overall National Command

Commander in Chief: President Ronald Reagan
Secretary of Defense: Caspar Weinberger
Chairman of the Joint Chiefs of Staff: Gen. John Vessey
Commander in Chief of Atlantic Command: Adm. Wesley McDonald

Joint Task Force 120

Commander: Vice Adm. Joseph Metcalf, Commander of Second Fleet
Deputy Commander: Maj. Gen. Norman Schwarzkopf (Army advisor to Metcalf outside chain of command until evening of Oct 26)

Task Force 123/Joint Special Operations Command (JSOC): Maj. Gen. Richard Scholtes

Army Rangers (transferred to Task Force 121 on evening of Oct 25)
    1st Battalion, 75th Infantry: Lt Col. Wesley Taylor – 350 Rangers (plus 100 Rangers in C Company detached for other missions on Oct 25 and 27)
    2nd Battalion, 75th Infantry: Lt Col. Ralph Hagler – 250 Rangers
Navy SEAL Team 6: Capt. Robert Gormly
    Reconnaissance of Point Salines (Oct 23–24 and 24–25): Lt Patrick Toohey – 22 operators
    Assault on Radio Free Grenada (Oct 25): Lt Donald (Kim) Erskine – 12 operators
    Rescue of Governor-General Scoon (Oct 25–26): Lt Wellington (Duke) Leonard – 22 operators
Delta Force: Col. Sherman Williford
    Assault on Richmond Hill Prison (Oct 25): Maj. Richard Malvesti (A Squadron), Maj. David Grange (B Squadron) – 44 operators
Task Force 160/160th Aviation Battalion: Lt Col. Terence Henry – nine Black Hawk helicopters, 45 pilots and crew

Task Force 124/Amphibious Squadron 4, US Navy: Capt. Carl Erie

Flagship: USS *Guam* (helicopter carrier)
Support ships: USS *Barnstable County*, USS *Fort Snelling*, USS *Manitowoc*, USS *Trenton*
22nd Marine Amphibious Unit (MAU): Col. James Faulkner – 1,700 Marines
    Battalion Landing Team 2/8 (2nd Battalion, 8th Marines): Lt Col. Ray Smith – 822 Marines
    Marine Medium Helicopter Squadron 261 (HMM-261): Lt Col. Granville Amos – 21 helicopters, 57 pilots and crew
Navy SEAL Team 4: Lt Michael Walsh – six operators

Task Force 121/82nd Airborne Division, US Army: Maj. Gen. Edward Trobaugh

2nd Brigade: Col. Stephen Silvasy
    2nd Battalion, 325th Infantry: Lt Col. Jack Hamilton – 730 paratroopers
    3rd Battalion, 325th Infantry: Lt Col. John Raines – 730 paratroopers
    2nd Battalion, 508th Infantry: Lt Col. Ralph Newman – 730 paratroopers (arrived Oct 28)
3rd Brigade: Col. James Scott
    1st Battalion, 505th Infantry: Lt Col. George Crocker – 730 paratroopers
    2nd Battalion, 505th Infantry: Lt Col. Keith Nightengale – 730 paratroopers
    1st Battalion, 508th Infantry: Lt Col. Hubert Shaw – 730 paratroopers

Task Group 20.5/*Independence* Carrier Battle Group, US Navy: Rear Adm. Richard Berry

Flagship: USS *Independence* (aircraft carrier)
Support ships: USS *Caron*, USS *Clifton Sprague*, USS *Coontz*, USS *Moosbrugger*, USS *Richmond K. Turner*

Military Airlift Command (MAC), US Air Force (supporting JTF 120 but not under its command): Brig. Gen. Robert Patterson

Caribbean Peacekeeping Force (supporting JTF 120 but not under its command) – 353 soldiers and policemen

Overall Commander: Brig. Rudyard Lewis, Chief of Staff of Barbados Defence Force
Ground Commander: Col. Ken Barnes, Jamaica Defence Force
    Jamaica contingent – 152 soldiers
    Barbados contingent – 60 soldiers, 50 policemen
    Antigua and Barbuda contingent – 14 soldiers
    Dominica contingent – 15–20 policemen
    St Lucia contingent – 15–20 policemen
    St Kitts and Nevis contingent – five policemen (only three deployed to Grenada)
    St Vincent and the Grenadines contingent – 15–20 policemen (arrived Oct 29)

GRENADA

People's Revolutionary Armed Forces

Commander: Gen. Hudson Austin, Chairman of the Revolutionary Military Council (RMC), Minister of Defence and Interior
Deputy Commander: Lt Col. Ewart Layne, Vice Chairman of the RMC, Deputy Minister of Defence

People's Revolutionary Army (PRA) – 463 soldiers mobilized (906 official total strength)

Motorised Company: Lt Raeburn Nelson – 148 soldiers, 15 militiamen, seven armored personnel carriers, two armored scout cars
Mobile Company: Lt Raeburn Nelson – 102 soldiers
Exploration Company: Lt Callistus Bernard (Iman Abdullah) – 106 militiamen
Security Platoons: Capt. Lester Redhead – 28 soldiers, 43 militiamen (forming a single company); 54 soldiers, 23 militiamen (detachments distributed to various posts)
Antiaircraft Battery: Lt Cecil Prime – 46 soldiers, four militiamen

People's Revolutionary Militia (PRM) – 257 militiamen mobilized (2,500 official total strength)

St George's Battalion (Military Region I): Lt Col. Ewart Layne (incorporated into PRA units)
St David's Battalion (Military Region I): Lt Col. Ewart Layne (incorporated into PRA units)
St Andrew's Battalion (Military Region II): Lt George
St Patrick's Battalion (Military Region III): Maj. David Bartholomew
Carriacou Battalion (Military Region IV): Lt Callistus Bernard (Iman Abdullah)

CUBA

Cuban Forces

Commander: Col. Pedro Tortoló Comas, Chief of Staff of Army of the Center

Military advisors to Grenadian armed forces – 43 total

Construction workers/military reservists – 636 total

US strategic plan of attack and Grenadian–Cuban defenses

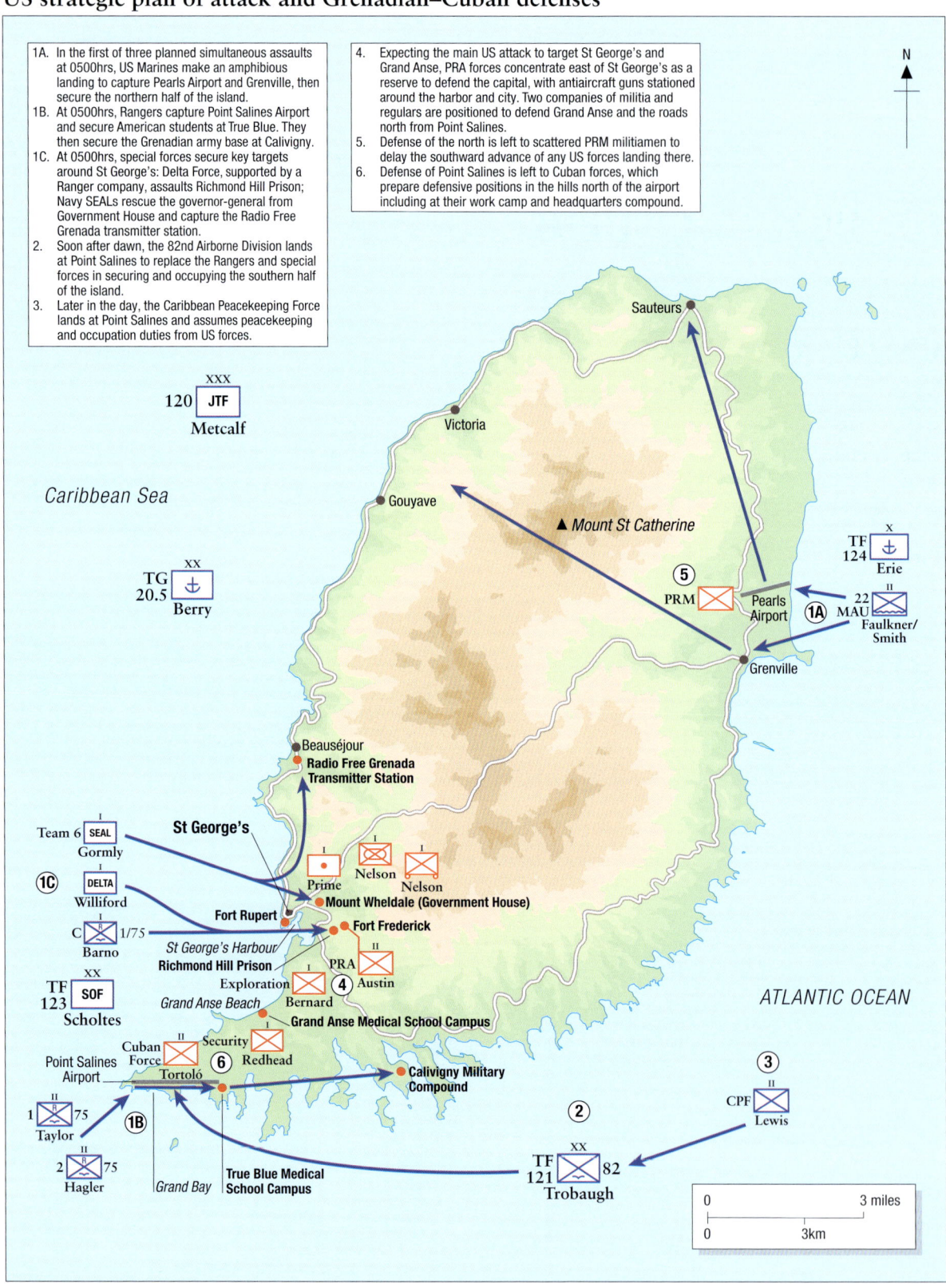

1A. In the first of three planned simultaneous assaults at 0500hrs, US Marines make an amphibious landing to capture Pearls Airport and Grenville, then secure the northern half of the island.

1B. At 0500hrs, Rangers capture Point Salines Airport and secure American students at True Blue. They then secure the Grenadian army base at Calivigny.

1C. At 0500hrs, special forces secure key targets around St George's: Delta Force, supported by a Ranger company, assaults Richmond Hill Prison; Navy SEALs rescue the governor-general from Government House and capture the Radio Free Grenada transmitter station.

2. Soon after dawn, the 82nd Airborne Division lands at Point Salines to replace the Rangers and special forces in securing and occupying the southern half of the island.

3. Later in the day, the Caribbean Peacekeeping Force lands at Point Salines and assumes peacekeeping and occupation duties from US forces.

4. Expecting the main US attack to target St George's and Grand Anse, PRA forces concentrate east of St George's as a reserve to defend the capital, with antiaircraft guns stationed around the harbor and city. Two companies of militia and regulars are positioned to defend Grand Anse and the roads north from Point Salines.

5. Defense of the north is left to scattered PRM militiamen to delay the southward advance of any US forces landing there.

6. Defense of Point Salines is left to Cuban forces, which prepare defensive positions in the hills north of the airport including at their work camp and headquarters compound.

N

Caribbean Sea

ATLANTIC OCEAN

XXX
120 | JTF
Metcalf

Sauteurs

Victoria

Gouyave

▲ Mount St Catherine

XX
TG 20.5 | ⚓
Berry

⑤
PRM

Pearls Airport

Grenville

X
TF 124 | ⚓
Erie

II
22 MAU
①A
Faulkner/ Smith

Beauséjour
Radio Free Grenada
Transmitter Station

I
Team 6 | SEAL
Gormly

St George's

①C | DELTA
Williford

C | 1/75
Barno

I
Prime

I
Nelson

I
Nelson

Fort Rupert
Mount Wheldale (Government House)

Fort Frederick

St George's Harbour
Richmond Hill Prison

XX
TF 123 | SOF
Scholtes

Exploration
Bernard

Grand Anse Beach

II
PRA
④ Austin

Grand Anse Medical School Campus

Cuban
Force
Tortoló

II
⑥

I
Security
Redhead

Point Salines
Airport

II
1 75
Taylor

①B

II R
2 75
Hagler

Grand Bay

Calivigny Military
Compound

②

③

II
CPF
Lewis

XX
TF 121 | 82
Trobaugh

True Blue Medical
School Campus

0   3 miles

0   3km

OPPOSING PLANS

UNITED STATES

Operation *Urgent Fury* came as a surprise to the Reagan administration and the US military. American commanders were given little notice and an exceptionally compressed time frame to plan a complex undertaking that involved every branch of the US military. This joint operation, the first major combat deployment of the post-Vietnam all-volunteer force, required close coordination between the Army, Navy, Marines, Air Force, and special forces. In both its innovations and its flaws, the campaign on Grenada became a model for unexpected contingency missions whose legacy extended into the post-Cold War era.

The Pentagon fashioned a military plan that would rely on two critical factors – speed and surprise – to capture Grenada with a *coup de main*, achieving victory with a swift knockout blow. The concept for the operation was to overwhelm the defenders by rapidly capturing key targets before the Grenadian or Cuban armed forces had time to mount a substantial opposition. To minimize friction and organizational confusion between the different services involved, planners divided the island into two sectors: a northern half assigned to the Marines and a southern half given to the Army and special forces. Meanwhile, a naval battle group centered on the aircraft carrier USS *Independence* would cordon off the island and provide surface and air support, while the Air Force would transport troops and supplies from bases in the US and Barbados and provide further air support to the ground forces.

Gen. John Vessey briefs congressional leaders on the plans for Operation *Urgent Fury* in the Cabinet Room of the White House on the morning of October 25, 1983. (Courtesy Ronald Reagan Presidential Library)

The first phase of the main invasion of Grenada was intended to deliver the knockout punch – capturing the island's strategic points, subduing resistance, and securing several hundred stranded American medical students as quickly as possible. Success relied on three separate assaults from units of different military branches occurring simultaneously:

1) Marines from Amphibious Squadron 4 would make an amphibious

21

landing on beaches near Pearls Airport on Grenada's northeast coast, then would capture the airport and the nearby port town of Grenville, pushing inland to secure the northern half of the island.

2) Meanwhile, Army Rangers flying directly from bases in the continental United States would land on the larger runway under construction at Point Salines at Grenada's southwestern tip, prepared to parachute if conditions required. They were tasked with seizing the airport, then advancing to secure the American medical students at the True Blue campus of St George's Medical School located less than 100 yards from the runway's eastern edge. Their final objective was to assault and secure the main base of the Grenadian army at Calivigny, further east from the medical school campus along the island's southern coast.

3) Finally, special forces flying by helicopter from Barbados were tasked with three secret and sensitive missions around St George's, aimed at securing Grenada's democratic political future. First, two squadrons of Delta Force operators, supported by a company of Rangers, would assault Richmond Hill Prison to free political prisoners of the regime. Second, a force of Navy SEALs would rescue Grenada's governor-general, Sir Paul Scoon, from house arrest at his residence, Government House. Third, a smaller force of Navy SEALs would capture the Radio Free Grenada transmitter station at Beauséjour north of St George's to allow the rescued Scoon to deliver a broadcast to the Grenadian people and the international community.

This spearhead of the invasion relied on stealth for success, and the simultaneous arrival in darkness of these three forces from their widely spread starting points – Marines from ships offshore, Rangers from bases in the US, and special forces from Barbados – would be essential to successfully capture all of the critical targets. While planners initially set 0200hrs as the coordinated time for all forces to begin the attack, logistical problems pushed this planned launch time back to 0500hrs, less than an hour before daybreak. The challenges of executing such a complex coordinated assault with so little room for error in its timing would plague the operation from the beginning.

With these key missions accomplished, the second phase of the operation would begin not long after dawn. A large force of paratroopers from the 82nd Airborne Division would land at Point Salines and take over responsibility for the southern half of the island from the Rangers and special forces. As the invasion's reserve force, the paratroopers would

Intelligence shortcomings plagued the planning for Operation *Urgent Fury* and greatly contributed to the challenges US forces faced on the ground. US troops did not possess detailed or up-to-date maps of Grenada, some having to rely on tourist maps. (National Archives)

mop up any remaining resistance and establish order within this more populous half of Grenada, linking up with and eventually taking over from the Marines advancing from the island's less populated northern half. Later on the initial day of the operation, the third phase called for US forces to begin handing over peacekeeping duties across the island to the military and police units from America's coalition partners that formed the Caribbean Peacekeeping Force. These Caribbean coalition partners played no role in the planning of the operation.

GRENADA

In the aftermath of the coup against Maurice Bishop, the leaders of the RMC had to improvise a defense against invasion with the meager forces at their disposal from the PRA and the PRM. Following Bloody Wednesday and Bishop's execution, the RMC and PRA high command relocated their headquarters from Fort Rupert in St George's to Fort Frederick on a ridge to the east of the capital. This colonial-era stone fortress became the command center for Grenada's military forces during the campaign.

The RMC was surprisingly well informed about American intentions, if not the specifics of the invasion plan US forces would carry out. As early as the evening of October 23, the RMC broadcast a warning on Radio Free Grenada that soldiers from Caribbean nations and other "foreign forces" were gathering on Barbados to launch a military intervention on Grenada. Having failed to avoid confrontation through diplomatic means or to enlist more robust Cuban military assistance, the RMC prepared to defend against an American invasion. The PRA would have at its disposal only a fraction of its official military strength, as the government's call for nationwide mobilization had mustered a pitiful response: only half of the army's regular soldiers and just one in ten of its militia had answered the call to service. With this meager manpower, the RMC leadership decided to concentrate its defenses in the strategically valuable southwest of the island. Defense of the north would be left to whatever militia forces rallied to the call to arms; militiamen would man the two antiaircraft guns at Pearls Airport and mount a delaying action against any enemy forces that landed there.

In the southwest, the RMC predicted with relative accuracy which key points the invaders would target, assuming that the Americans would direct their attacks toward Point Salines and St George's. RMC planners anticipated that the Americans would mount amphibious and possibly helicopter landings with air and naval support at St George's Harbour, Grand Anse Beach, and potentially Grand Bay south of the Point Salines runway. They accordingly positioned the PRA's main strike force – the Motorised Company with its armored vehicles and the Mobile Company – to the east of St George's with the task of defending the capital and acting as a reserve force for other endangered fronts nearby. Meanwhile, the PRA's Exploration Company was tasked with the defense of the Grand Anse area south of St George's. A final company formed from a mix of militia and regulars in PRA security platoons took up position to block the roads leading north from Point Salines to St George's. Finally, the RMC recognized that the antiaircraft defense of St George's would play a crucial role in the coming battle and stationed antiaircraft guns at Fort Rupert, Fort Frederick, and Frequente. Defense of Point Salines would be left to the Cubans.

CUBA

Cuba's lukewarm support for Grenada's new hardline Marxist government contradicted the assumptions of American planners and dashed the hopes of Grenadian leaders. Fidel Castro made clear that he would keep Cuba's support for the new Grenadian regime at arm's length. Castro condemned the bloody coup against his protégé Maurice Bishop, realizing that this blunder had given the US an ideal pretext to invade. Nevertheless, having committed vast resources to assist the Grenadian socialist revolution, he did not want to completely abandon his ideological ally to its fate.

Castro refused to send military reinforcements to Grenada for the practical reason that American naval and air dominance in the Caribbean made doing so "impossible and unthinkable." Moreover, he severely limited the rules of engagement under which the Cubans would fight, restricting Cuban involvement in the coming military campaign to a defensive role. He ordered Cuban personnel to fire on the Americans "only if we are directly attacked," in which case the Cubans should "vigorously defend" their ground as if it were Cuban soil. Otherwise, the Cubans should not interfere with American efforts to evacuate their citizens from the medical school nearby. He justified this balancing act as a way of "defending ourselves, not the [Grenadian] Government or its deeds."

Castro sent an experienced officer, Col. Pedro Tortoló Comas, to oversee Cuban defensive preparations and ensure that his restrictive orders were understood and carried out. Castro rejected the RMC's requests to coordinate military planning and withdrew Cuban military advisors from the PRA units to which they had been assigned. In effect, the Cubans would operate completely independently from the Grenadian military forces, under separate leadership, rules of engagement, and areas of operation. The Cubans, not Grenadian forces, controlled the ground defensive positions around Point Salines Airport, and they placed obstacles on the runway with construction equipment, trucks, and metal stakes joined by wire.

Castro's restrictive orders undermined any effective military defense, limiting the discretion and flexibility of Cuban forces to respond to a potential invasion while demanding that they mount vigorous resistance if attacked. As it turned out, the Cubans on the ground at Point Salines did not follow their leader's orders to the letter. While the Cubans' initial response to the landing of American forces was restrained, captured workers later admitted that some in their ranks took the initiative in firing upon the Americans.

Castro ordered Cuban forces to prepare defensive positions around their work and living camps on the Point Salines peninsula, including the "Old Camp" north of the airport. The Cubans lacked time to complete substantial entrenchments and dug only modest trenches at both of their camps. (National Archives)

THE CAMPAIGN

WEEKEND OF CRISIS

It was supposed to be a relaxing golfing weekend – an escape from the trials and tribulations of Washington. Instead it became the weekend that brought the two gravest national security crises of President Ronald Reagan's first term in office.

Secretary of State George Shultz had invited Reagan to spend the weekend at the Augusta National Golf Club in Georgia, where the President would stay in the Eisenhower Cottage, built for his predecessor several decades earlier. Reagan had left for Georgia knowing that storm clouds were gathering over the Caribbean, but he decided to proceed with the long-planned trip to maintain an air of normalcy, bringing along his new national security advisor, Robert "Bud" McFarlane, to oversee any critical developments.

Officials at the White House had met for the first time to discuss the deepening crisis in Grenada the day before Reagan left for his trip. In the aftermath of the violent coup and the murder of Maurice Bishop, they had grown increasingly concerned that the anarchy that seemed to prevail on the island would continue in a downward spiral. On the recommendation of the crisis management team chaired by Vice President George H. W. Bush, the President ordered the Pentagon to redirect two naval battle groups, including USS *Independence* and an amphibious squadron carrying a contingent of Marines bound for Lebanon, toward Grenada to monitor the evolving situation. The next day, prior to leaving for Augusta, Reagan signed the official order approving contingency planning for a possible military intervention.

In the early-morning hours of Saturday, October 22, 1983, Reagan was awakened with word that the OECS, comprising Grenada's closest neighbors in the region, had formally requested American participation in a multinational military intervention to restore order and democracy to Grenada. Reagan and his advisors knew that OECS leaders had held an emergency meeting in Barbados the night before to discuss the situation in Grenada, which they called an "unprecedented threat to the peace and security of the region." Now a diplomatic cable arrived sharing the news that the OECS member states (except Grenada) had unanimously resolved to form a multinational Caribbean force "to depose the outlaw regime on Grenada by any means, including intervention by force of arms," and requested assistance from the United States as well as Britain, Jamaica, and Barbados.

Awakened in the middle of the night on October 22, 1983, President Reagan, still clad in his pajamas, gathers with Secretary of State George Shultz (center) and National Security Advisor Bud McFarlane (left) in the living room of the Eisenhower Cottage to discuss the urgent OECS request for military intervention on Grenada. (Courtesy Ronald Reagan Presidential Library)

After an early morning conference call connecting the Eisenhower Cottage with the White House Situation Room and a shorter phone discussion with his top advisors later in the morning, Reagan gave preliminary approval to move forward with a military operation. As Shultz recalled, "President Reagan's reaction was decisive. What kind of a country would we be, he asked, if we refused to help small but steadfast democratic countries in our neighborhood to defend themselves against the threat of this kind of tyranny and lawlessness?" Reagan later reflected that "there was only one answer I could give to McFarlane and Shultz and those six countries who asked for our help." He saw it as his duty to rally to the defense of democracy, particularly so close to America's shores, and he also feared the Cold War strategic threat that a communist stronghold under Cuban or Soviet control would pose to American interests.

Reagan was also concerned over the deteriorating situation in Grenada for an even more immediate and pressing reason: the presence of nearly 600 American citizens who were living on the island as medical students. Prior to the 1979 Grenadian revolution, a group of American investors had founded St George's University School of Medicine in 1976. Despite some tensions, the Bishop regime recognized the school's economic benefits for the island and allowed the capitalist enterprise to maintain its operations. Nevertheless, the presence of so many American citizens on Grenada prompted fears within the Reagan administration that the new hardline Marxist government, under duress and fearing invasion, might seize hostages from among the vulnerable student body – a potential nightmare scenario reminiscent of the Iran hostage crisis only a few years earlier that had torpedoed the presidency of Reagan's predecessor. With "the searing memory of Tehran" fresh in mind, Reagan and his team of advisors were determined to avoid a similar fate.

Shultz in particular feared that conditions were "ripe" for hostage-taking and urged action, while Bush and Secretary of Defense Caspar Weinberger counseled taking more time to gather information. But the President made his decision clear. Responding to McFarlane's assurance that the Pentagon could prepare a rescue mission within 48 hours, Reagan said simply, "Do it." As he recounted in his diary later that evening, "I've OK'd an outright invasion."

But Reagan's weekend only grew more tumultuous. As the presidential party neared the end of its golf outing that afternoon, a gunman crashed his pickup truck through the gates of Augusta National and took hostages in the pro shop, demanding to meet with the President. Reagan, surrounded by his Secret Service detail, tried unsuccessfully to connect with the gunman by phone. The man released the hostages and was arrested several hours later.

More devastating developments lay ahead. On Sunday, October 23, Reagan was awakened in the middle of the night for the second day in a row with the tragic news that terrorists had bombed the US Marine barracks in Beirut, Lebanon, killing 241 American servicemen. With any thoughts of golf now gone, Reagan returned immediately to the White House for a day full of meetings with his National Security Council (NSC) in the Situation Room to discuss the simultaneous crises in Grenada and Lebanon – the first top secret and the second public. Despite later claims from critics that the tragedy in Beirut prompted Reagan to launch the Grenada operation to distract public attention, the opposite in fact proved the case, as the NSC discussed the possibility of canceling or delaying the Caribbean intervention to turn fully instead to the bloodshed in the Middle East. However, on the basis of fresh intelligence reports that persuaded him that the American students on Grenada were in imminent danger, Reagan reaffirmed his decision to move forward with the military operation.

As he weighed the appeal for intervention from the coalition of Caribbean nations, Reagan had to decide on the objectives of the coming campaign. Originally envisioned by Pentagon planners as a non-combat rescue mission to evacuate American nationals, the possibility was growing stronger by the day that the violent regime and anarchic conditions on Grenada would not allow American forces to land without a fight. The OECS request for assistance and Reagan's own strategic preference to reverse communist advances in the Caribbean pointed to the wisdom of a more ambitious mission

President Reagan meets with his national security team in the White House Situation Room to discuss the simultaneous crises in Grenada and Lebanon on October 23, 1983. Reagan decided to expand the ultimate objective of the mission from evacuating Americans to regime change against Grenada's violent communist leadership. (Courtesy Ronald Reagan Presidential Library)

aimed at regime change in Grenada to restore democratic government to the island nation. Reagan was inclined toward the overall goal of regime change and disarming Grenada as early as October 22, when he first learned of the OECS request. Asked by Bush for his views on the operation's ultimate objective, Reagan replied that "if we've got to go there, we might as well do all that needs to be done."

Throughout the weekend, Reagan's team of advisors set to work on drafting the official presidential order to execute the mission, which would outline the central goals of the campaign. This highly classified document, called National Security Decision Directive (NSDD) 110A, laid out three principal objectives for the American-led military intervention: 1) protecting the endangered American citizens on Grenada, 2) restoring order and democracy to the people of Grenada, and 3) eliminating Cuban intervention on the island nation. NSDD-110A directed the Pentagon to "land U.S. and allied Caribbean military forces in order to take control of Grenada, no later than dawn Tuesday, October 25, 1983." D-Day and H-Hour were now set to launch the multinational, multi-service campaign to capture Grenada.

Later in the evening of October 23, after an exhausting day of meetings to deliberate on the ongoing crises, McFarlane brought the finalized copy of NSDD-110A upstairs to the White House residence, briefing the President on the latest intelligence from the Caribbean. For the final time, Reagan reviewed the official presidential order to send American troops into battle. Then, without hesitation, he pulled a pen from his pocket and signed the document. President Reagan had one word for his national security advisor: "Go."

INITIAL MOVES: PLANS AWRY

Just as Reagan was signing the presidential order to execute the operation on the evening of October 23, the first components of the mission were unraveling with tragic results. Navy SEAL Team 6, in its first combat test since its creation as an elite and clandestine counterterrorist unit in the aftermath of the failed hostage rescue in Iran in 1980, was tasked with a reconnaissance mission to land on Grenadian beaches and assess conditions at Point Salines Airport. In particular, the SEALs' assignment was to determine whether conditions on the runway under construction were suitable for the landing of American military aircraft carrying the Ranger assault force that would capture the airport on the morning of the invasion, or whether obstacles would require the Rangers to make a parachute landing instead.

Because the mission was assigned at such short notice, 16 SEALs would parachute from Air Force transports carrying them from their base in the US to rendezvous with their assault team leader, Lt Patrick Toohey, along with five more SEALs aboard USS *Clifton Sprague*, part of the *Independence* carrier battle group positioned 40 miles offshore from Grenada. The full team of 22 commandos would then travel to Grenadian shores in two Boston Whaler boats specially rigged for the parachute drop.

This complex plan fell apart almost immediately. Told to expect a daylight jump into calm seas, the SEALs opening their planes' cargo ramps instead found darkness and an unexpected squall that brought heavy rain and a rough ocean below. The original drop time had been delayed to 1800hrs to allow the planes to take a more circuitous route to avoid detection from Cuban electronic surveillance. But this delay did not take into account the time zone and daylight savings time differences that meant darkness would fall an hour earlier in Grenada than in the eastern United States. Four SEALs drowned in the stormy seas and darkness, likely weighed down by their heavy parachutes and equipment load, and one of the Boston Whalers sank. This would be one of the deadliest episodes for American forces in the entire campaign, yet it had not even officially begun.

The surviving SEALs joined their comrades and attempted to carry out their mission in the one Boston Whaler left. But as they evaded what they thought was a Grenadian patrol vessel on their way toward Grenadian shores, the boat took on water and lost one engine. Postponing their reconnaissance until the next night, the eve of the invasion, the commandos set off for Grenada once again, this time with a second boat that had been airdropped to replace the one that had been lost. Once again, however, the vessels took on water in the heavy seas and the SEALs were forced to abort their mission when they could not restart their engines in time to reach the Grenadian coast before the main invasion force would arrive at daybreak.

Navy SEALs undertook two clandestine reconnaissance missions in the days leading up to the invasion. Stormy seas prevented SEAL Team 6 from reaching Point Salines and caused four to drown, but SEAL Team 4 successfully scouted the beach approaches to Pearls Airport. (Mike Leahy, Navy Art Collection, Naval History and Heritage Command)

At the same time on the night of October 24, as the second unsuccessful attempt to reconnoiter Point Salines Airport was turned back in frustration, another SEAL team met with greater success on the opposite side of the island. Six commandos from Navy SEAL Team 4, under the command of Lt Michael Walsh, were attached to the amphibious squadron carrying the Marines who would launch the attack on Pearls Airport, Grenada's small commercial airfield on its northeast coast, the next morning. As the squadron approached Grenadian shores, the SEAL team set out to scout the suitability of the beach at the eastern end of the Pearls runway for the planned amphibious landing. They did not like what they found: while the beach itself was suitable for landing craft, the approach to it passed through a coral reef with rough surf. Walsh radioed his report back to the squadron, prompting the Marines to shelve their plans for an amphibious landing in favor of a helicopter assault. Their mission complete, the six SEALs took refuge in foxholes on the beach, where they waited for morning and the attack that would accompany first light.

DAY 1: URGENT FURY, UNDER SIEGE

The American public learned that American soldiers, sailors, and Marines had gone into battle for the first time since the Vietnam War at 0907hrs on the morning of October 25, when President Reagan strode into the White House Press Briefing Room. Alongside him was Eugenia Charles, the prime minister of Dominica and chairman of the OECS who had championed the multinational intervention. Together, these two leaders announced the start of the military operation – as Reagan described it, "a joint effort to restore order and democracy on the island of Grenada."

Prime Minister Eugenia Charles of Dominica (right), the anticommunist chairman of the OECS, meets with President Reagan, George Shultz (left), and Bud McFarlane in the Oval Office on October 25, 1983. Her resolute role in orchestrating and justifying the operation proved critical in shaping how the American public and the rest of the world viewed the military campaign. (Courtesy Ronald Reagan Presidential Library)

Charles proved particularly adept and effective in justifying the military action to the press, vigorously denying that the operation was an offensive invasion or an act of aggression. She emphasized that the island states of the eastern Caribbean, with their shared history and intermixed populations, were "one region – we belong to each other, are kith and kin" to a greater extent than typical sovereign nations, and therefore "Grenada is part and parcel of us." She argued that the intervention was "a question of our asking for support" since "we don't have the capacity, ourselves, to see to it that Grenadians get the freedom that they're required to have to choose their own government." Charles made the same forceful case in briefings with congressmen and consultations in the Oval Office with Reagan, Shultz, and the rest of the cabinet.

By the time of these public pronouncements, however, the action on the ground in Grenada was already well underway, and indeed the first phase of the fighting was nearly complete.

First ashore: Marines capture Pearls and Grenville

The spearhead of the initial American assault was supposed to pierce Grenada's defenses in three places simultaneously. Instead, each of these attacks occurred piecemeal, as logistical challenges stymied their coordination and forced them all behind schedule.

The first blow fell where Grenadian defenses were weakest: at the sparsely defended Pearls Airport. This regional commercial airport was situated on the island's northeast coast near the port town of Grenville, Grenada's second-largest town after St George's. Though American planners expected to meet a stout defense at this strategic point, the Grenadian regime left the defense of this part of the island to the handful of local militiamen who answered the call to arms.

Of the three initial invasion forces, the Marines launched their assault from the closest proximity to the island, based 10 miles offshore on the ships of Amphibious Squadron 4. Helicopters from HMM-261 would ferry them to their landing zones near Pearls and Grenville. Lt Col. Granville Amos,

Day 1 of Operation *Urgent Fury*, October 25, 1983

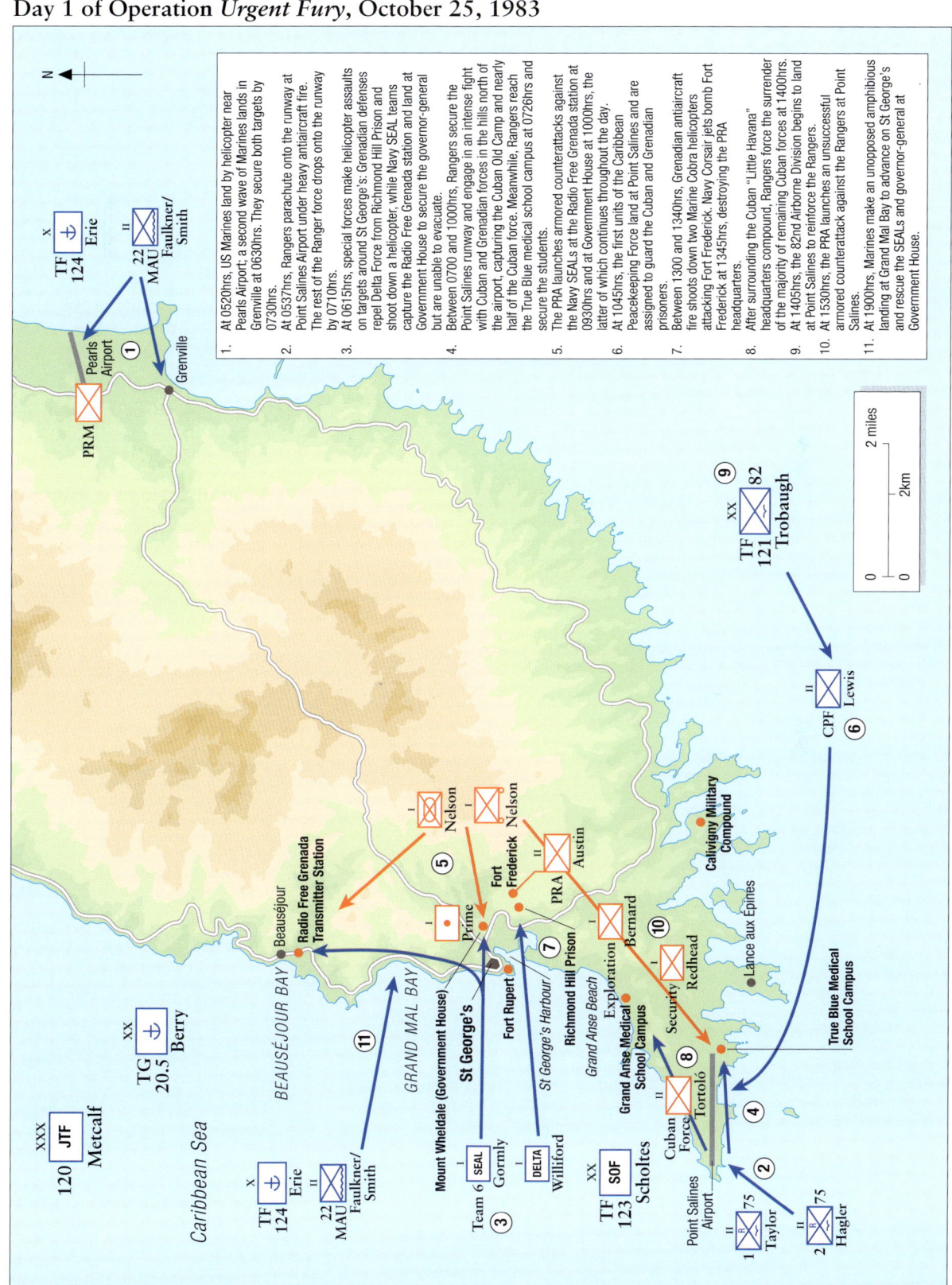

1. At 0520hrs, US Marines land by helicopter near Pearls Airport; a second wave of Marines lands in Grenville at 0630hrs. They secure both targets by 0730hrs.

2. At 0537hrs, Rangers parachute onto the runway at Point Salines Airport under heavy antiaircraft fire. The rest of the Ranger force drops onto the runway by 0710hrs.

3. At 0615hrs, special forces make helicopter assaults on targets around St George's: Grenadian defenses repel Delta Force from Richmond Hill Prison and shoot down a helicopter, while Navy SEAL teams capture the Radio Free Grenada station and land at Government House to secure the governor-general but are unable to evacuate.

4. Between 0700 and 1000hrs, Rangers secure the Point Salines runway and engage in an intense fight with Cuban and Grenadian forces in the hills north of the airport, capturing the Cuban Old Camp and nearly half of the Cuban force. Meanwhile, Rangers reach the True Blue medical school campus at 0726hrs and secure the students.

5. The PRA launches armored counterattacks against the Navy SEALs at the Radio Free Grenada station at 0930hrs and at Government House at 1000hrs, the latter of which continues throughout the day.

6. At 1045hrs, the first units of the Caribbean Peacekeeping Force land at Point Salines and are assigned to guard the Cuban and Grenadian prisoners.

7. Between 1300 and 1340hrs, Grenadian antiaircraft fire shoots down two Marine Cobra helicopters attacking Fort Frederick. Navy Corsair jets bomb Fort Frederick at 1345hrs, destroying the PRA headquarters.

8. After surrounding the Cuban "Little Havana" headquarters compound, Rangers force the surrender of the majority of remaining Cuban forces at 1400hrs.

9. At 1405hrs, the 82nd Airborne Division begins to land at Point Salines to reinforce the Rangers.

10. At 1530hrs, the PRA launches an unsuccessful armored counterattack against the Rangers at Point Salines.

11. At 1900hrs, Marines make an unopposed amphibious landing at Grand Mal Bay to advance on St George's and rescue the SEALs and governor-general at Government House.

In 1983, Pearls Airport was a rundown aviation facility that consisted of a 5,151ft runway suitable only for turboprop planes with under 50 passengers, as well as a small cinderblock terminal and fuel storage site. (National Archives)

Marine helicopters launch from USS *Guam* and its support ships to begin the predawn attack on Pearls Airport. The complex process of loading and refueling the helicopters on the flight decks occurred in pitch darkness and driving rain, causing delays. (Mike Leahy, Navy Art Collection, Naval History and Heritage Command)

at the helm of HMM-261, would command the landing before turning over battlefield command to Lt Col. Ray Smith. Smith's Battalion Landing Team 2/8, 822 Marines strong once all ashore, would be the first ground troops to set foot on Grenadian soil and begin the invasion.

Once again, bad weather caused delays. The full force of 21 helicopters did not finally lift off from the deck and begin its short journey to the island until 0500hrs, the designated H-Hour for the landings. The original plan to land on the runway at Pearls had been scrapped for fear of the damage that defensive firepower could inflict from the hills surrounding the airfield. Instead, the Marines chose a landing zone several hundred yards to the south of the airport on what was labeled on their maps as an old unused racetrack. What they actually found was an overgrown field filled with palm trees, some as tall as 60ft. Forced to improvise, the lead helicopter touched down in a clearing at the edge of the field.

The double-rotor CH-46 Sea Knight helicopters carrying the Marines and the single-rotor CH-53 Sea Stallions ferrying their vehicles and heavy supplies followed the lead of the first successful landing and touched down at 0520hrs, 20 minutes late but well ahead of the other elements of the invasion force. This first wave of the Marine assault was relieved to find their landing completely unopposed. But all would not remain so tranquil for long.

As the follow-up waves of Marine helicopters approached the improvised landing zone, antiaircraft guns from the hills overlooking Pearls from the north opened fire. The two 12.7mm guns were manned by Grenadian militiamen wearing T-shirts and shorts. As the sun began to rise and

visibility improved, the militia gunners set their sights on the airborne targets, with one female gunner excitedly shouting to her loader, "Keep feeding me!" Fortunately for the Marines, their aim was poor and their fire caused no damage. The attack helicopters escorting the Marines, two AH-1T Sea Cobra gunships, promptly silenced the guns and dispersed the militia. This opening exchange of fire, first from Grenadian militia and then from the Cobra helicopters, marked the official start of hostilities, with no casualties on either side.

Marines from the 22nd Marine Amphibious Unit land just south of Pearls Airport to begin the invasion. The initial landing faced minimal opposition from Grenadian militia and resulted in no casualties for either side. (Mike Leahy, Art Collection, National Museum of the Marine Corps)

Once on the ground, the Marines wasted no time in advancing toward their objectives. While one platoon secured the perimeter of the landing zone and other Marines wrestled with unloading tangled equipment from a Sea Stallion helicopter, Lt Col. Smith advanced with two platoons toward the airfield. They breached a chain-link fence near the terminal, drawing some scattered small-arms fire from militia defenders who quickly fled to the west. Fearing that Grenadian troops had re-manned the antiaircraft position atop the hill overlooking the runway, Smith ordered one of the attacking platoons to seize the high ground to the north. As the Marines advanced toward them, the militia gunners again fled their posts without firing, leaving behind their weapons and a small stockpile of munitions. As the Marines consolidated their position around the airport terminal, they came under scattered mortar fire from the west but suffered no casualties before the Grenadian militia once more abandoned their weapons. Fighting around Pearls Airport had ceased.

At 0630hrs, around the same time the Marines reached the airport, a second wave landed unopposed in Grenville, capturing the major town on

The Marines attacking Grenville landed on a soccer field surrounded by a high brick wall that was vulnerable to defending fire, but the pilots correctly gambled that this landing would also face little opposition. The Marines quickly secured the town. (National Archives)

Grenada's east coast 2 miles to the south of Pearls. Once again, palm trees unexpectedly obstructed the planned landing zone, so Lt Col. Amos in the lead chopper made the decision to land instead on a large soccer field in the middle of town. This second landing also faced little opposition, and the Marines were greeted with an enthusiastic welcome from Grenadian civilians, who cheered them as liberators from the oppressive RMC rather than invaders. Indeed, the civilians spent the rest of the day leading the Marines to hidden weapons caches in the town and pointing out Grenadian militiamen and soldiers who had shed their uniforms in an attempt to avoid capture by blending in with the population.

By 0730hrs, after dispersing token resistance from Grenadian militia, the Marines declared both Pearls Airport and Grenville to be secure. There were no reported casualties on either side of the fighting. Establishing the Pearls airfield as a base of supply, the Marines left their own imprint on the airport terminal, hanging a handmade sign over the entrance to rename it "Marine Corps Air Station Douglas" in memory of a revered sergeant major who had been killed in the terrorist bombing in Beirut two days earlier.

Parachuting under fire: Rangers seize Point Salines and True Blue

The Army Rangers shouldered the heaviest burden of the fighting on all three days of battle. They were tasked with two of the most critical missions of Operation *Urgent Fury* on the first morning of the invasion: the capture of the military-grade airport under construction at Point Salines and the rescue of the American students at the True Blue medical school campus located nearby. The plans drawn up at the Pentagon envisioned the Rangers' role to be limited to serving as the spearhead of the invasion – to seize the most vital strategic points on Grenada and then hand over the remaining mop-up and stabilization duties to the larger follow-on force of paratroopers from the 82nd Airborne Division before the end of the first day. Instead, the Rangers found themselves at the center of the action through October 27, given many of the most challenging missions and facing some of the most intense combat of the battle for Grenada.

After the failure of the Navy SEALs to reconnoiter the condition of the Point Salines runway, the Rangers were forced to rely on aerial surveillance photographs of the airfield and the surrounding terrain and Cuban positions. (Courtesy Ronald Reagan Presidential Library)

AIRFIELD UNDER CONSTRUCTION
POINT SALINES, GRENADA

10,000 FOOT RUNWAY

FUEL STORAGE

NEW CUBAN HOUSING

The Air Force ferried the two Ranger battalions to Grenada in an armada of 24 transport and escort aircraft from four different military airfields in the southern United States. The complexity of the airlift plan stood in contrast with that of the Marines based on ships just offshore and caused significant delays. The voyage of 2,300 miles from the Rangers' staging ground at Hunter Army Airfield in Savannah, Georgia, to the drop zone at Point Salines took seven and a half hours – a long and uncomfortable trip for the troopers packed shoulder-to-shoulder in the cargo bays of the C-130 Hercules transport planes carrying them into combat. Upon receiving news from

This aerial view of the Point Salines peninsula shows the exceptional narrowness of the Rangers' drop zone on the runway, surrounded by water on three sides. To make matters even more dangerous, the Rangers' planes encountered thunderstorms with rain and stiff winds as they approached Grenadian shores. (National Archives)

the pilot of an AC-130 Spectre gunship that the runway was obstructed with construction vehicles and other smaller obstacles, the commander of the lead Ranger battalion, Lt Col. Wesley Taylor, made the decision for all of his troopers to parachute onto the runway rather than land directly in their planes as originally planned.

A last-minute malfunction of the lead plane's navigational equipment forced Maj. Gen. Richard Scholtes, the commander of the special operations forces that included the Rangers, to reorganize the order of the planes that would make the assault, causing a delay that pushed the Rangers' arrival back by 30 minutes. By that time, the Marines had already made their landing near Pearls Airport and the shooting had started – surprise was thus lost. The Rangers were flying toward one of the most heavily fortified parts of the island defended by an enemy that expected their attack.

But the one factor in the Rangers' favor was the fact that Grenadian and Cuban forces expected an amphibious assault on Point Salines rather than a parachute drop. They had fortified the beach to the south of the runway to defend what they knew would be a prime target for the American invaders, and the antiaircraft guns in the hills to the north of the airport were positioned to fire on aircraft at higher altitude. Taylor, the commander of the 1st Battalion whose plane would be the first to drop, made the bold decision that his troopers would make their jump from the exceptionally low altitude of 500ft, less than half the normal height and too low for the use of reserve parachutes if the main chutes failed. Risky as it was, this plan would minimize the Rangers' exposure to enemy fire and chances of dropping off course into the ocean.

The first wave of Rangers approached the coast of Grenada from the west, passing over the length of the runway from the side that opened toward the sea. The Grenadian defenders were prepared, locking a searchlight onto the lead plane and prompting the Air Force pilot to lament to his co-pilot, "I don't think this is going to be a big surprise." From a height lower than the Washington Monument, the first Rangers leapt through the rear cargo door of their plane. No sooner had the dim early morning sky filled with parachutes than a torrent of antiaircraft fire, red and green tracer bullets, and small-arms fire lit up the brightening dawn with an intensity that the pilot

Capture of Point Salines Airport and True Blue campus, October 25, 1983

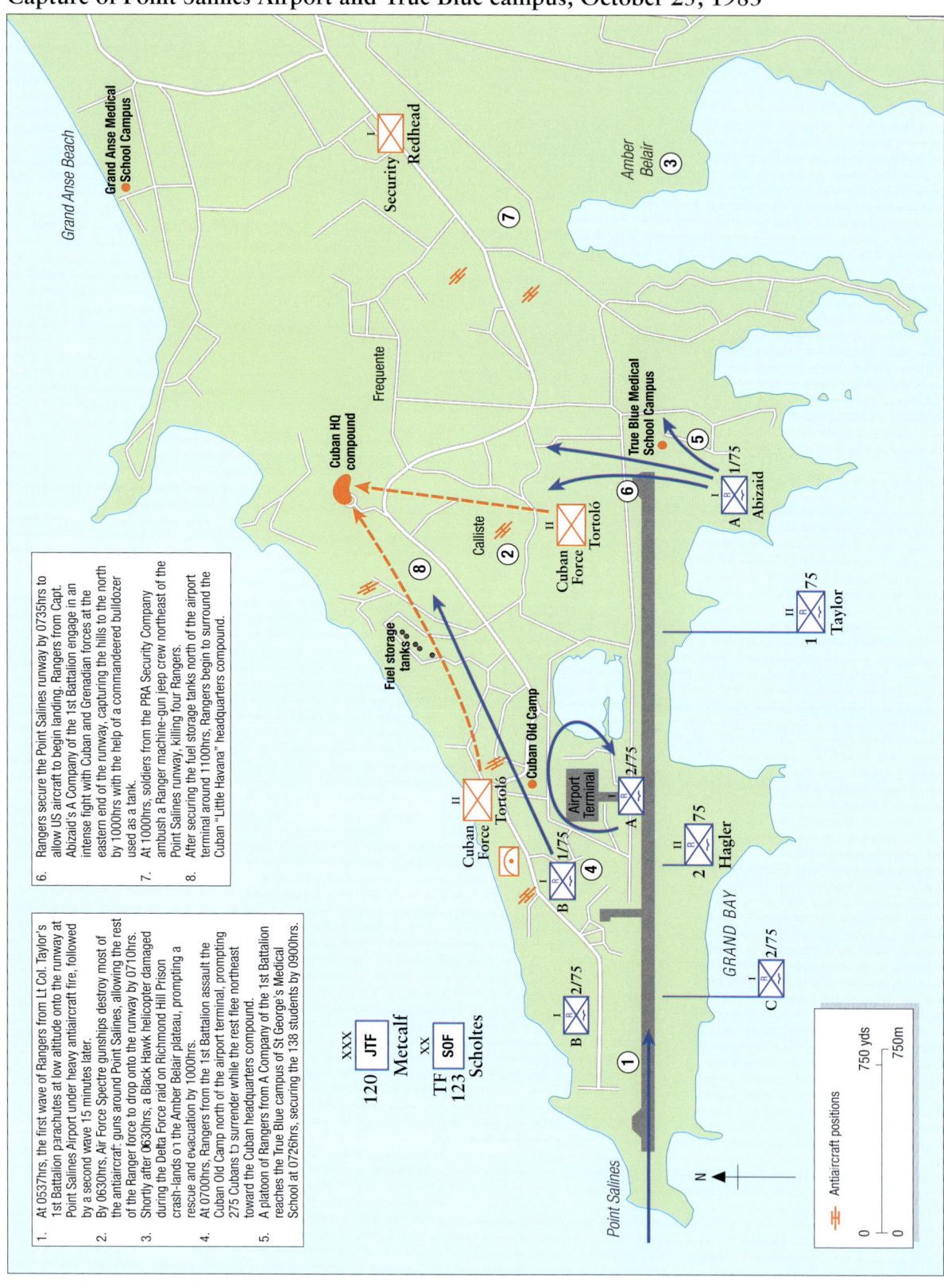

1. At 0537hrs, the first wave of Rangers from Lt Col. Taylor's 1st Battalion parachutes at low altitude onto the runway at Point Salines Airport under heavy antiaircraft fire, followed by a second wave 15 minutes later.

2. By 0630hrs, Air Force Spectre gunships destroy most of the antiaircraft guns around Point Salines, allowing the rest of the Ranger force to drop onto the runway by 0710hrs.

3. Shortly after 0630hrs, a Black Hawk helicopter damaged during the Delta Force raid on Richmond Hill Prison crash-lands on the Amber Belair plateau, prompting a rescue and evacuation by 1000hrs.

4. At 0700hrs, Rangers from the 1st Battalion assault the Cuban Old Camp north of the airport terminal, prompting 275 Cubans to surrender while the rest flee northeast toward the Cuban headquarters compound.

5. A platoon of Rangers from A Company of the 1st Battalion reaches the True Blue campus of St George's Medical School at 0726hrs, securing the 138 students by 0900hrs.

6. Rangers secure the Point Salines runway by 0735hrs to allow US aircraft to begin landing. Rangers from Capt. Abizaid's A Company of the 1st Battalion engage in an intense fight with Cuban and Grenadian forces at the eastern end of the runway, capturing the hills to the north by 1000hrs with the help of a commandeered bulldozer used as a tank.

7. At 1000hrs, soldiers from the PRA Security Company ambush a Ranger machine-gun jeep crew northeast of the Point Salines runway, killing four Rangers.

8. After securing the fuel storage tanks north of the airport terminal around 1100hrs, Rangers begin to surround the Cuban "Little Havana" headquarters compound.

of the next plane likened to the Fourth of July fireworks show over the National Mall in Washington, DC. The largest American parachute drop into a combat zone since World War II was underway.

The first Rangers hit Grenadian soil on the eastern half of the runway at 0537hrs. Remarkably, they landed without suffering any casualties or injuries, though six had holes in their parachutes from navigating through the heavy fire flying around them on their descent. They did not realize that they were facing two separate forces at Point Salines, with Grenadian soldiers manning the antiaircraft guns and Cubans firing small arms from their defensive positions north of the runway. Neither of these defensive forces was initially effective, which accounted for the Rangers' safe passage through the air: the Grenadian antiaircraft guns were not able to lower their barrels far enough to target the incoming planes, while Castro's order for Cuban forces to fire only if attacked – though widely disobeyed in practice – did keep the hostile welcome they offered the Rangers from being as deadly as it might otherwise have been.

This aerial view shows the unfinished runway at Point Salines looking east, as the Rangers' planes approached it on the morning of October 25, with the airport terminal and Cuban and Grenadian defenses to the left and the open ocean to the right. (National Archives)

The first planeload of Rangers to land on the runway was about 40 men strong, over a third of which included Taylor and his battalion headquarters staff rather than the runway clearing teams that were supposed to have landed first. The following planes in the first wave were driven off by ground fire when they attempted to make their drops, being forced to reorganize before they could make another pass. In the meantime, for the first 15 minutes, Taylor and his men were alone. The lead platoon took up a defensive position on high ground just to the north of the runway while Taylor set up his command post in a roofless concrete building to the south. As they dug in and waited for reinforcements, the second planeload of Rangers finally parachuted onto the Point Salines runway at 0552hrs.

The antiaircraft fire against this second wave was at least as intense as the first, coming primarily from two Grenadian-manned and Soviet-made ZU 23mm guns positioned near the PRA supply depot at Frequente to the northeast of the airport. These guns fired explosive rounds the size of golf balls, which could be seen from the bridge of USS *Guam*, the flagship of Joint Task Force 120 commander Vice Adm. Joseph Metcalf, on the opposite side of the island. From this perch, Maj. Gen. Norman Schwarzkopf anxiously watched what he later described as "a cone of red and green tracer fire" that passed just over the top of the planes and parachuting Rangers, who floated to the ground while dodging fire "from all sides on the ground." He admitted: "I can't recall any combat operation that the United States has ever been involved in that could have been more intense than that."

This painting shows the Rangers' parachute drop from the perspective of the Grenadian antiaircraft guns in the hills to the north of the airport. The low-altitude approach of the planes protected the parachuting Rangers from the heavy antiaircraft fire from the guns, which were not able to lower their barrels enough to target the incoming Americans. (Mike Leahy, Navy Art Collection, Naval History and Heritage Command)

RANGERS' PARACHUTE ASSAULT ON POINT SALINES AIRPORT, 0552HRS, OCTOBER 25, 1983 (PP.38–39)

US Army Rangers were tasked with capturing the most critical targets of Operation *Urgent Fury*: the military-grade airport under construction at Point Salines and the nearby medical school campus at True Blue with its contingent of American students. Learning that a series of obstacles blocked the runway (1), Lt Col. Wesley Taylor, the commander of the 1st Battalion, ordered his Rangers to make a parachute landing at low altitude on the narrow peninsula, surrounded by ocean on three sides.

From a height of only 500ft, Taylor's lead plane dropped its Rangers under heavy fire from Cubans defending the hills to the north of the runway and antiaircraft guns manned by Grenadian soldiers in the hills to the north and northeast of the airport (2). This fire drove off the remaining planes transporting the rest of the Ranger force. For the first 15 minutes from when they began their landing at 0537hrs, Taylor's initial wave of 40 Rangers was the only American force on the ground. Taylor set up a command post to the south of the runway (3) while his men began taking up defensive positions (4).

While Cuban fire against the Rangers on the ground intensified, the planes made their second attempt to offload the remaining force. As the lead C-130 Hercules approached the runway at 0552hrs (5), a storm of antiaircraft fire enveloped it in a cone of red and green bullets that lit up the brightening predawn sky (6). This second wave of parachuting Rangers descended through the hail of fire onto and around the runway (7). Remarkably, no Americans were killed or injured by enemy fire, since the Grenadian guns had been positioned to fire on aircraft flying at a higher altitude and thus overshot their targets. They nevertheless succeeded in driving off the follow-on planes once again.

This second planeload of Rangers bolstered the American position around the runway, but these 80 soldiers remained alone and outnumbered until after 0630hrs, when Air Force Spectre gunships destroyed most of the Grenadian antiaircraft guns and allowed the rest of the Ranger force to land with far less resistance. The assault on Point Salines was the largest American combat parachute drop since World War II.

Once again, the intense ground fire drove off the follow-up planes and prevented them from dropping the rest of the Ranger force. To make matters worse, a miscommunicated order from Taylor on the ground to the ten remaining transport planes led the rest of the Ranger force to prepare to land on the runway rather than parachute. The cumbersome process of re-rigging the Rangers to airdrop added to the delays. For the first hour, Taylor and his meager force of about 80 Rangers had to hold out against intensifying fire from the Cubans, who controlled the defenses to the north of the airport.

Two Air Force Spectre gunships, with heavy cannon and machine gun firepower, finally tilted the odds in the Rangers' favor. These powerful variants of the C-130 aircraft carrying the Rangers into battle silenced most of the ground fire around the airport and destroyed the majority of the Grenadian antiaircraft guns in the vicinity by 0630hrs. Wasting no time, and now encountering only minor resistance, the remaining ten transport planes were able to airdrop the rest of the Ranger force between 0634hrs and 0710hrs. The green parachutes of the Rangers filled the now-bright morning sky. The full initial invasion force of Rangers, nearly 500 strong, took up positions around the runway, though it took some time for the intermingled units to sort themselves out. Taylor's 1st Battalion assembled on the eastern half of the runway, while the newly arrived 2nd Battalion, commanded by Lt Col. Ralph Hagler, took responsibility for the runway to the west of the control tower and terminal buildings.

While the large-scale parachute drop was still underway, the Rangers on the ground began preparations to accomplish their two key objectives:

Once Air Force Spectre gunships had destroyed the Grenadian antiaircraft guns around the airport, the full force of Rangers was able to complete its parachute drop facing little resistance, in contrast to the hail of fire that met the first Rangers to land on the Point Salines runway. (US Army)

US forces used the open ground to the south of the runway as a staging ground for operations around Point Salines Airport. While some Rangers advanced on the Cuban Old Camp north of the terminal (both visible at center), others battled the Cuban and Grenadian defenders in the hills east of the terminal. (National Archives)

securing the area around the airport and rescuing the medical students from the nearby campus. By 0700hrs, Rangers from the 1st Battalion began advancing on the Cuban "Old Camp," a complex of 22 barracks buildings located on a hill immediately to the north of the airport terminal. A three-man team of Rangers, closely followed by the rest of the first platoon to land on the runway, began the assault on the defensive positions around the barracks compound, killing two Cubans and capturing 28 prisoners. Supported by snipers and machine guns, the rest of the platoon then attacked the camp from the west. Before the assault could get fully underway, a flood of Cuban construction workers emerged from their barracks to surrender after offering little resistance, leaving behind their weapons and military gear. In all, the platoon of Rangers captured about 275 Cuban prisoners, while the rest fled their overrun camp toward the Cuban headquarters compound, "Little Havana," near the village of Calliste to the northeast.

After the capture of the Cuban Old Camp and the completion of the Ranger parachute drop, the focal point of combat shifted to the eastern end of the runway. There, Capt. John Abizaid gathered the Rangers in his A Company of the 1st Battalion at an assembly point near Taylor's command post south of the runway. Abizaid, known to his men as "the Mad Arab" for his Lebanese descent, was a West Pointer respected for his improvised tactical skills who would later come to greater prominence as the top US commander in the Middle East during the height of the Iraq War. Abizaid assigned two of his platoons to clear the runway of obstacles and secure the hilly ground to the north that they labeled "Goat Hill," from where a mixed force of Cubans and Grenadians were firing on them across the runway. As they started to move out, a dump truck containing two PRA soldiers roared down the eastern end of the runway. After halting the vehicle and disarming its occupants, the Rangers learned that the Grenadian soldiers had simply been trying to make a routine delivery, apparently unaware that an invasion was happening.

The fight for the eastern end of the runway soon escalated into a pitched battle that, according to Taylor, was "at least as intense as any of the fights I was in in Vietnam." The Rangers suffered their first casualty – Specialist Mark Yamane, the first American combat death on Grenadian soil – when the captured dump truck came under heavy fire from Goat Hill, stalling their advance across the runway. With help from a Spectre gunship overhead, which pummeled the building that had been the source of the fire on the truck, the Rangers began to work their way across the runway. Echoing John Wayne's heroics in the World War II movie *The Fighting Seabees*, Abizaid's men used a commandeered Cuban bulldozer as a tank to advance under fire and capture the hills. With its shovel extended as a shield against enemy fire, several Rangers drove the bulldozer across the runway and up the hill to the north as their squad followed behind,

This aerial view shows the Point Salines runway looking west. In the foreground is the eastern end of the runway that became the focus of the heaviest combat on the morning of October 25, as Capt. Abizaid's Rangers crossed the runway under fire to capture the hills to the north (visible on the right). (National Archives)

one soldier riding from a perch behind the dozer's blade. As the momentum of the battle shifted toward the advancing Rangers, the Cubans retreated north to the Little Havana compound while the Grenadians dispersed to the northeast. By 1000hrs, Abizaid and his A Company completed their capture of the hills and occupied the high ground north of the runway.

While the battle raged for the eastern end of the airfield, the rest of the Ranger force worked to clear the runway of obstructions to allow US aircraft to begin landing. By 0735hrs, the Rangers had finished clearing the runway and declared it to be secure. The first aircraft landed minutes later to offload vehicles, supplies, and reinforcements. Among the first to land was Scholtes's command plane, which the general then left behind to establish his ground headquarters in the airport terminal at the center of the runway, from which he could more easily oversee the ongoing missions around Point Salines and St George's.

Meanwhile, the third platoon of Abizaid's A Company slipped along the shoreline south of the runway toward the medical school campus located in a hollow north of True Blue Bay, just past the eastern end of the runway. The small campus of St George's Medical School was surrounded by a chain-link fence and included five dormitories, a lecture hall, cafeteria, and basketball court. The Rangers reached the campus at 0726hrs, encountering only token resistance from the handful of Grenadian soldiers guarding the campus gates, who quickly dispersed upon hearing the Americans approach. By 0900hrs, the Rangers declared the campus and 138 students secure.

But just as it seemed that one of the central goals of the operation had been accomplished without a hitch, the Rangers learned some shocking news that upended US military plans for the rest of the operation: True Blue was not in fact the main campus of St George's Medical School, and only a fraction of its students lived there. The main campus, along with more than two-thirds of the medical students, was located at Grand Anse about 2 miles away in a larger compound along Grenada's most picturesque beach. The Grand Anse campus lay between Point Salines and St George's, behind enemy lines well to the north of the current Ranger positions near the airport. This unexpected development came as startling news to the Rangers on scene and to the American commanders offshore, and reverberated up the chain of command to Washington. Without question, this amounted to the most significant intelligence failure of the operation.

Although the Rangers had rescued the American students at True Blue, the majority of US civilians on Grenada remained out of reach and in harm's way for another day. For now, there was nothing the Rangers could do.

The Cubans blocked the Point Salines runway with dump trucks, bulldozers, and other obstacles. Finding keys still in the ignition of the construction vehicles, the Rangers were able to simply drive them off the runway, while one trooper used an asphalt roller to flatten steel rods. (National Archives)

When the Rangers reached the student dorms at the True Blue campus of St George's Medical School around 0830hrs, the students met the approaching American soldiers with cheers and relief. But they also shared some unexpected and startling news: the main campus and most students were located elsewhere. (National Archives)

SPECIAL OPERATIONS MISSIONS AROUND ST GEORGE'S, OCTOBER 25–26, 1983

US special forces, including Navy SEALs and Delta Force, launched a series of missions around the capital city of St George's aimed at securing Grenada's political future, but they ran into fierce resistance from Grenadian antiaircraft fire and armored counterattacks.

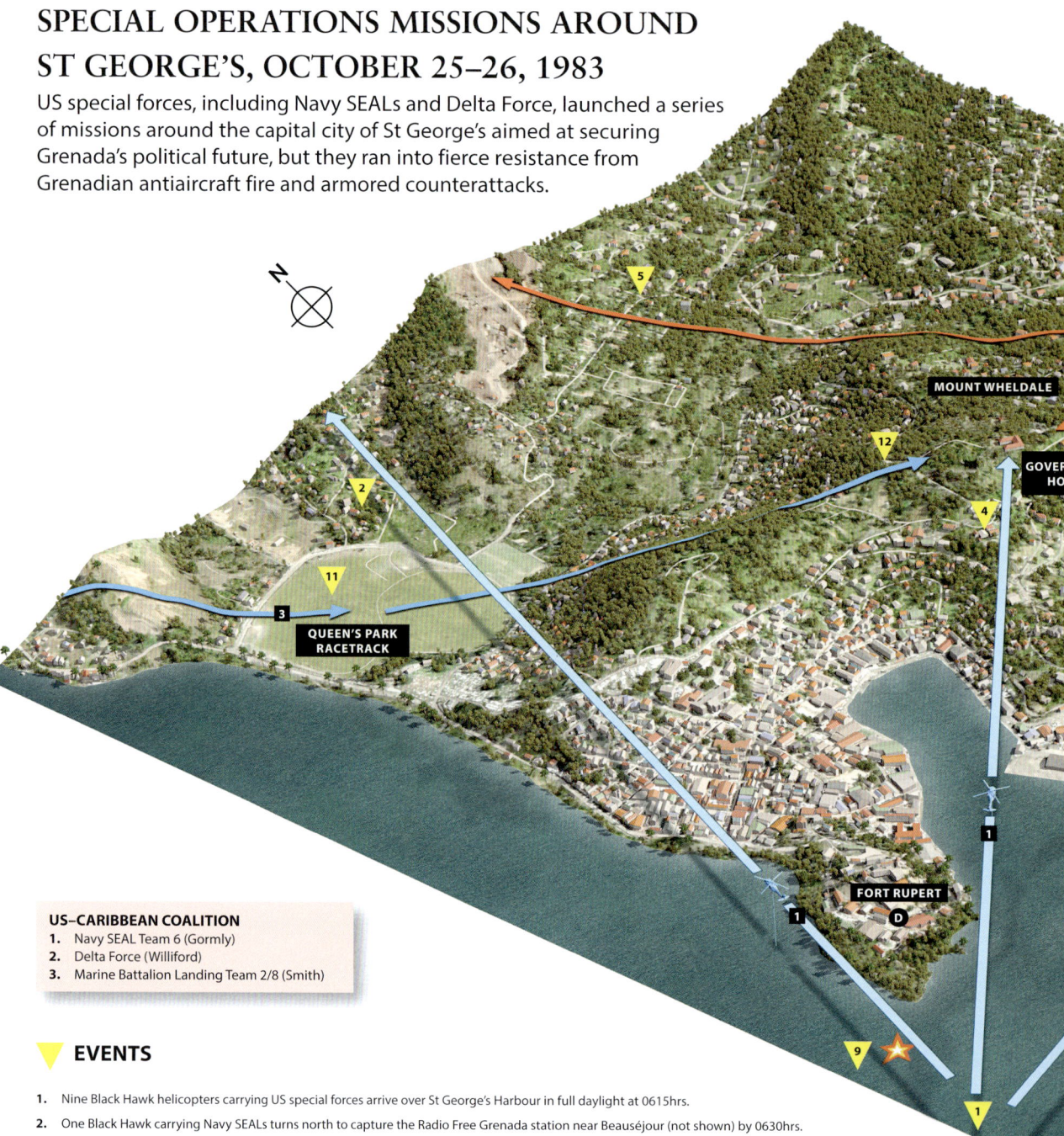

MOUNT WHELDALE

GOVERNMENT HOUSE

QUEEN'S PARK RACETRACK

FORT RUPERT

US–CARIBBEAN COALITION
1. Navy SEAL Team 6 (Gormly)
2. Delta Force (Williford)
3. Marine Battalion Landing Team 2/8 (Smith)

▼ EVENTS

1. Nine Black Hawk helicopters carrying US special forces arrive over St George's Harbour in full daylight at 0615hrs.

2. One Black Hawk carrying Navy SEALs turns north to capture the Radio Free Grenada station near Beauséjour (not shown) by 0630hrs.

3. PRA antiaircraft guns at Fort Frederick repel the six Black Hawks carrying Delta Force squadrons to Richmond Hill Prison, shooting down one helicopter which crashes on the southern coast (not shown).

4. Navy SEALs land at Government House to secure the governor-general, but heavy fire drives off the two helicopters and prevents evacuation.

5. A PRA counterattack at 0930hrs forces the SEALs to abandon the radio station and escape to Navy ships offshore.

6. PRA infantry and APCs launch a pincer counterattack on Government House at 1000hrs, which is driven back by Spectre gunships at 1015hrs. The SEALs and Spectres repel renewed APC attacks around 1530hrs and 2215hrs.

7. At 1300hrs, two Marine Cobra helicopters attack Fort Frederick, but PRA antiaircraft guns shoot down one at 1327hrs.

8. After crashing in a field near the harbor, the pilot of the downed Cobra is rescued in another helicopter.

9. At 1340hrs, PRA antiaircraft fire shoots down the second Cobra as it covers the escape of the rescue helicopter; the downed Cobra crashes just outside St George's Harbour.

10. Navy Corsair jets bomb Fort Frederick at 1345hrs, destroying the PRA headquarters.

11. At 1900hrs, Marines land at Grand Mal Bay and advance overnight to establish a command post at the Queen's Park Racetrack.

12. At 0600hrs on October 26, Marines arrive at Government House to relieve the SEALs and bring the governor-general to safety.

Note: the base map covers an area of approximately 1.9 x 1.6 miles (3 x 2.5km).

GRENADA
A. PRA HQ (Austin)
B. Motorised Company (Nelson)
C. Mobile Company (Nelson)
D. Antiaircraft Battery (Prime)

FORT FREDERICK

RICHMOND HILL PRISON

BUTLER HOUSE

GEORGE'S HARBOUR

ROSS POINT

PRA HQ Austin

Nelson

Nelson

Prime

TF 123 **SOF** Scholtes

Team 6 **SEAL** Gormly

DELTA Williford

2 8 Smith

Through the maelstrom: Special operations missions around St George's

The most secret element of the initial American invasion plan was the trio of special operations missions that aimed to protect the Grenadians who could lead the way in restoring democracy to the island nation after the fighting had ended. The unexpectedly intense combat that the special forces faced in carrying out these missions produced some of the worst tragedies – as well as the most-storied heroics – of the entire campaign.

The Navy SEAL and Delta Force units that would go into action on Grenada arrived at their staging ground at the airport on Barbados in the predawn hours of October 25 after flying overnight from Fort Bragg in North Carolina. Like their Ranger counterparts in Gen. Scholtes's JSOC task force, the SEALs and Delta Force operators quickly fell behind schedule due to delays in unloading and preparing the UH-60 Black Hawk helicopters that would carry them into battle. The nine Black Hawks, flown by the specially trained "Night Stalker" pilots of the 160th Aviation Battalion, did not arrive over Grenada from Barbados until 0615hrs, 75 minutes later than planned and in full daylight rather than darkness. This loss of stealth and surprise posed an even graver problem for the special forces than it had for the parachuting Rangers, since the success of their sensitive missions hinged on slipping into and out of their targets virtually unnoticed. Though these units were made up of some of the US military's most skilled and highly trained soldiers, they were not equipped or prepared to face the intensity of opposition that awaited them.

By the time the nine Black Hawks reached the eastern shore of Grenada and then wrapped around the southern coast past Point Salines and on to the capital city – returning the waves of Marines who had just captured Pearls Airport and then watching the unfolding battle erupting across the Point Salines runway down below – the pilots and commandos knew they had lost any chance of launching a surprise attack. The dark green Black Hawks approached the harbor of St George's plainly visible in the full dawn light now that the early morning storms had passed. The majority of the PRA's

The Army's clandestine 160th Aviation Battalion, known as the "Night Stalkers" for its special training in nighttime flying, had to carry special forces to their targets around St George's in full daylight. Grenada marked the unit's first time in combat – and the first combat test for the newly designed UH-60 Black Hawk helicopters. (National Archives)

antiaircraft defenses were positioned at strategic points around the capital city and its harbor, lying in wait.

Just as they reached the coast near St George's, the ninth Black Hawk veered north to deposit its team of Navy SEALs at the radio transmitter station near Beauséjour. The other eight helicopters flew ahead into the interlocking field of fire that quickly enveloped them from guns around the mouth of the harbor. On their first pass over the city's buildings, the unexpectedly heavy fire caused the helicopters to miss their landmark on the ground that signaled the point where they would break into two groups to reach their separate targets. Several of the pilots and crew suffered wounds from the ground fire. After returning to sea, the choppers successfully found their landmark on the second pass, two heading northeast toward the governor-general's mansion while the remaining six turned southeast toward Richmond Hill Prison.

These six Black Hawks heading for the prison carried two Delta Force squadrons with 44 operators divided between them. Their objective was to free political prisoners of Grenada's communist regime from the fortress prison perched atop a high ridge to the southeast of the city. The steepness of the ridge and the height of the fortress walls, surrounded by dense jungle and undergrowth, did not offer any suitable landing zones and forced the Black Hawk pilots and Delta Force teams to improvise. The helicopters maneuvered to a position above the prison, where they would hover over the courtyard while the Delta Force commandos "fast-roped" to the ground. But in doing so as they approached the prison, the Black Hawks exposed themselves to a new maelstrom of fire from the Grenadian antiaircraft guns deployed to protect Fort Frederick, the operational headquarters of the PRA and Grenada's RMC regime. Fort Frederick with its antiaircraft guns sat atop a significantly higher ridgeline to the east of the prison that dominated Richmond Hill from across a deep valley. The Black Hawks' position proved untenable as they emerged from the fire over the harbor of St George's into an even more destructive hail of flak and bullets.

Just as they were about to drop their ropes into the prison courtyard, the Delta Force commandos noticed that the compound appeared to have already been abandoned and deserted. Knowing that they could not

St George's Harbour and Grenada's capital city as seen from Fort Rupert. Mount Wheldale with Government House is visible on the left; the ridge with Richmond Hill Prison is on the right; the sports field where the Marine Cobra helicopter later crash-landed is in front of the ridge at the far right. (Hum Images/ Universal Images Group via Getty Images)

Richmond Hill Prison proved a far more challenging target than it had seemed to Pentagon planners looking at maps, as the steep terrain and high fortress walls prevented an easy landing for the Delta Force squadrons. (National Archives)

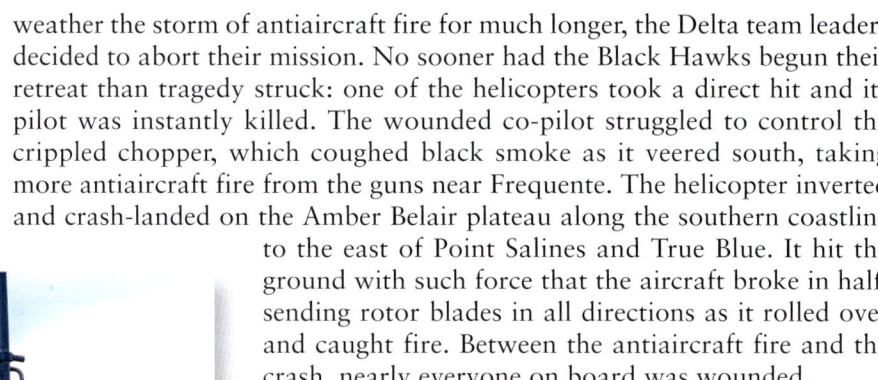

Grenadian forces positioned ten antiaircraft guns around St George's Harbour, including four Soviet-made ZU 23mm guns. The PRA's antiaircraft defenses proved far more effective and destructive at St George's than they had earlier at Pearls and Point Salines. (National Archives)

weather the storm of antiaircraft fire for much longer, the Delta team leaders decided to abort their mission. No sooner had the Black Hawks begun their retreat than tragedy struck: one of the helicopters took a direct hit and its pilot was instantly killed. The wounded co-pilot struggled to control the crippled chopper, which coughed black smoke as it veered south, taking more antiaircraft fire from the guns near Frequente. The helicopter inverted and crash-landed on the Amber Belair plateau along the southern coastline to the east of Point Salines and True Blue. It hit the ground with such force that the aircraft broke in half, sending rotor blades in all directions as it rolled over and caught fire. Between the antiaircraft fire and the crash, nearly everyone on board was wounded.

The plateau where the Black Hawk crashed was not easily accessible for evacuation, overgrown with jungle and vegetation and sitting atop steep cliffs with a rocky beach below. The other five Black Hawks, also damaged in the failed prison assault, flew out to sea in search of Navy ships on which they could offload their wounded. They then returned to the crash site, where Delta operators fast-roped onto the plateau to form a defensive perimeter around the downed helicopter and their wounded compatriots, holding off PRA soldiers with the help of a Spectre gunship overhead. A Navy SH-3H Sea King helicopter answered their mayday call and engineered an improvised rescue plan. The dense overgrowth on the plateau prevented the Sea King, a white-painted cousin of the Marine One helicopter that carried the President, from landing directly at the crash site. Instead, the survivors of the crash had to climb down the cliffs to the bay at the base of the plateau, where the amphibious Sea King touched down on the narrow shoreline with one landing wheel on the beach and the other in the surf. The Delta commandos waded out to the waiting rescue helicopter and climbed aboard. While the bay was shielded from enemy fire, it offered little room between the cliffs for the aircraft to maneuver. Only the skillful flying of the Sea King's pilot allowed the helicopter, now weighed down with its new passengers, to get airborne and make its escape by 1000hrs. The Delta Force assault on Richmond Hill Prison had ended in failure, with one helicopter shot down and its pilot killed. The human toll had been high, with an additional 18 Delta Force operators and several more air crew members wounded.

While Delta Force was running into unexpectedly stiff resistance at Richmond Hill Prison, the team of Navy SEALs in the Black Hawk that had separated from the rest to turn north was able to quickly accomplish its mission: the capture of the Radio Free Grenada station and its long-distance transmitter near the coastal village of Beauséjour, about 4 miles north of St George's. Finding their intended landing zone in front of the station blocked by farm equipment, the SEALs jumped off their Black Hawk in a meadow just to the northwest of the complex. Grenadian defenders began to fire on the landing helicopter as the Black Hawk maneuvered to shield the commandos and lay down covering fire from its side-mounted machine gun. The SEALs quickly closed on the station's cinderblock buildings, securing them as the Grenadians sped off in their truck at around 0630hrs.

Lt Donald "Kim" Erskine ordered his 12-man team to establish a defensive perimeter around the complex, including an ambush position along the main north–south road that ran past the radio station to the capital. The SEALs detained a Grenadian civilian family passing by in their

This aerial view of the Radio Free Grenada station near Beauséjour shows the tall radio transmitter and station buildings, the road leading south to St George's from which the later PRA counterattack came, the open meadow where the SEALs landed and across which they retreated, and the small jungle and river through which they escaped to the coastline. (National Archives)

car to prevent word of their presence from spreading. But this precaution became moot when about a dozen Grenadian militiamen drove up to the station at around 0900hrs in a Soviet-made military truck and several civilian vehicles. Erskine halted the convoy and ordered the Grenadians to drop their weapons, prompting a brief standoff that ended when one of the militiamen took cover behind a tractor and opened fire. The SEALs responded by unleashing a volley of fire that killed or wounded the entire band of Grenadians. The immediate threat eliminated, Erskine directed his team to turn the station into a field hospital and to set the civilian family loose now that the smoking Grenadian vehicles left no doubt of their presence.

The SEALs' mission at Beauséjour had been merely to briefly hold the radio station until their fellow commandos could bring the rescued governor-general of Grenada there to issue a broadcast to his nation. But with no word from the SEAL team sent to the governor-general's house – and finding their radio inoperable – Erskine and his men hunkered down to occupy the radio station indefinitely. One thing they knew for certain was that the Grenadian army was now aware of their exposed and isolated position. Uneasily, they settled down to await developments.

The final of the three special operations missions was the rescue of Governor-General Sir Paul Scoon from Government House, his official residence on Mount Wheldale just to the northeast of the capital city. This mission was the linchpin of the entire operation – the key to reestablishing democratic government on Grenada and justifying the military action before the international community. The planning for this covert operation called for a quick and little-noticed insertion of the main force of Navy SEALs, led by assault team leader Lt Wellington "Duke" Leonard and accompanied by the overall commander of SEAL Team 6, Capt. Robert Gormly. The SEALs would rapidly secure Government House and the governor-general, then immediately extract him to the Radio Free Grenada station to broadcast his support for the military intervention to his fellow countrymen and the world at large. None of this mission went according to plan.

Sir Paul Scoon represented – for both sides of the fighting, the RMC as well as the US-led coalition – constitutional authority in Grenada and therefore the legitimacy of a Grenadian government. His post as governor-general, which he had held since 1978, was a ceremonial one with no real political authority, but his dignified presence as the representative of Queen Elizabeth II – Grenada's head of state even after its independence from Britain in 1974 – signaled continuity and stability. For this reason, Maurice Bishop and Hudson Austin had each curried Scoon's favor after their respective coups, though Scoon, who prized Grenada's heritage of constitutional monarchy and parliamentary democracy, could not have been further apart ideologically from these socialist regimes.

While American claims were exaggerated that the RMC had placed Scoon under "house arrest" in the days

Governor-General Sir Paul Scoon represented legitimate constitutional authority on Grenada. His rescue was the linchpin of the American operation, as he would play the central role in restoring democracy and justifying the military intervention to the international community. (National Archives)

prior to the invasion, the governor-general was aware that the new regime kept his activities and calls under close surveillance. Asked by a visiting British diplomat on October 23 whether he would publicly support an American-led military intervention, Scoon expressed his fear that he "would probably be eliminated if he made any move that directly challenged the authority of the RMC" such as explicitly asking for "outside help." That said, Scoon made clear that if a Caribbean and American coalition undertook a military operation to restore stability to Grenada, he "would give such an initiative my fullest support," including with a formal written request once it was safe to do so. In the meantime, his implicit support for military intervention, conveyed orally, would have to suffice.

Scoon awoke soon after dawn on October 25 to the "zooming sound" of an aircraft overhead and the ringing of his telephone. "Your Excellency," his assistant told him, "the action has begun." Scoon rose from bed alongside his wife and briefly inspected the scene from his balcony, observing a helicopter under fire as it flew over St George's to the southwest. He then ordered his staff to take shelter in the basement of the elegant three-story mansion that served as his home and office.

The two Black Hawk helicopters carrying the Navy SEAL team swooped low over Government House and hovered over the grounds on either side of the mansion. Immediately, they began taking ground fire from the antiaircraft guns positioned at Fort Frederick on the ridge nearby and from PRA soldiers firing AK-47s from their positions around the official residences of Coard and the deceased Bishop next door to Government House. The SEALs in the helicopter to the mansion's front fast-roped out of their hovering Black Hawk, only to tumble through the trees and vegetation of the governor-general's steeply sloped front garden, while those in the chopper to the mansion's rear found an easier time roping down onto the tennis court that had once seen matches between Scoon and Bishop. This second Black Hawk continued to hover over the grounds with Capt. Gormly, his radio operator, and three US diplomats inside while they waited for the SEALs on the ground to use chainsaws to cut a landing zone from the brush to allow the civilians to safely dismount.

As the helicopter hovered, it was raked by what was later tallied up to 48 hits from ground fire. Maneuvering away from the close-quarters AK-47 fire from PRA troops on the ground, the Black Hawk exposed itself to antiaircraft fire from Fort Frederick, taking a direct hit that exploded through the cockpit floor to wound the lead pilot. As the co-pilot struggled to regain control, the careening aircraft veered away from Government House toward St George's Harbour, where it took more antiaircraft fire from guns placed at Fort Rupert. The co-pilot steadied the helicopter just in time to prevent it from crashing into the water. He ignored the entreaties of Gormly to return to Government House, instead taking the battered chopper out to sea to land on the deck of USS *Guam*, where the wounded pilot could receive medical attention. The Black Hawk was so badly damaged that flight deck crewmen had to douse its engines with hoses to shut them down. Gormly, for his part, was forced to accept transportation to establish a makeshift headquarters next to Gen. Scholtes in the Point Salines Airport terminal, from where he could attempt to monitor and aid his SEAL teams from afar.

Meanwhile, Lt Duke Leonard took charge of the team of 22 commandos on the ground at Government House. As the PRA soldiers retreated from

Government House, the elegant mansion that served as Governor-General Scoon's official residence and office on the outskirts of St George's, became a focal point of the fighting on October 25 as the PRA launched multiple armored counterattacks against the besieged Navy SEALs. (National Archives)

the environs of the property, the SEALs took up defensive positions in and around the mansion, spaced out in teams of two behind whatever cover they could find on the grounds while some chose perches on Government House's numerous balconies. Leonard took a group of his men indoors to seek out Scoon. Hearing the SEALs approaching, Scoon directed his staff to show themselves and reassured his wife that the soldiers were Americans and not Russians as she feared. One of his staffers opened the cellar door to find a commando pointing a gun directly at him. The SEALs confirmed Scoon's identity using photos of him that they carried around their necks, then set about protecting the governor-general and his party of ten, clearing the house of any hidden threats.

But the lull in the fighting outside was short-lived. As Government House became the target for PRA bullets, Leonard decided to move the governor-general and his wife to the mansion's interior dining room as the safest sanctuary from enemy fire, a choice whose wisdom was confirmed when a rifle-fired grenade exploded in one of the vacant sitting rooms. With no sign of their helicopters for a quick extraction and only short-range radios to make sporadic contact with Gormly at Point Salines, the embattled SEALs maintained a vigilant perimeter around Government House, waiting for a backup plan to take shape.

Counterattack: The PRA responds

Gen. Austin and the Grenadian high command monitored the flow of the morning's battles from their command post located in a bunker deep within the stone fortress of Fort Frederick. By 0800hrs, the PRA leadership at the fort was aware of the locations and vulnerabilities of American forces on the ground. They took the initiative during the brief lull in the fighting that followed the initial American landings to mount two concerted counterattacks to try to reverse the course of the ongoing battle. It was the actions undertaken by Grenadian military forces – not the Cubans – in the mid-morning of October 25 that shaped the trajectory of the rest of the campaign.

Having already written off any hope of effectively defending the area around Pearls Airport in the north, the PRA focused its counterattacks on the two areas where American forces were most isolated and vulnerable: the Radio Free Grenada station near Beauséjour and the governor-general's mansion on Mount Wheldale. To carry out its attacks, the PRA leadership decided to break off detachments from the PRA's main strike force, the infantry battle group that combined the Motorised Company with its armored vehicles and the Mobile Company with its trucks. This force, approximately 250 strong and under the command of Lt Raeburn Nelson, was stationed as a reserve in the hills to the east of St George's. Though the capital did not come under direct assault as the PRA had anticipated, Nelson's force was ready to respond to the nearby endangered points targeted by American special forces.

But first, the PRA sought to contain the American advance around Point Salines Airport in a handful of smaller clashes that were not directed from the military headquarters. Around 1000hrs, a machine-gun jeep crew, five Rangers strong from Capt. Abizaid's A Company of the 1st Battalion, was tasked with securing a road junction about a mile to the northeast of the runway and True Blue. The jeep was forced to circle back after the Rangers' imprecise map caused them to miss a turn. A group of Grenadian soldiers from Capt. Lester Redhead's company of mixed PRA and PRM units, guarding the roads leading away from Point Salines, lay in wait to ambush the unsuspecting Rangers. A shoulder-launched rocket-propelled grenade (RPG) destroyed the jeep, and three of the Rangers were killed immediately in the hail of Grenadian fire that followed. The remaining two Rangers sought cover on the opposite side of the wrecked jeep. While one laid down covering fire that killed at least one Grenadian soldier, the second Ranger managed to escape and make his way back to the main Ranger force near True Blue. He was hit multiple times, while his fellow Ranger was killed in the exchange of fire.

By mid-morning, the advance of the Rangers who had captured the high ground north of the eastern end of the runway with the help of a Cuban bulldozer had lost steam. Recoilless rifle fire from Little Havana drove Abizaid's troopers from A Company off Goat Hill around noon. The Rangers were able to quickly regain their lost position, however, when Metcalf – communicating with Scholtes and Taylor from offshore – authorized Marine Cobra attack helicopters to venture outside the Marines' sector of the island to aid the Army and special forces units in the south. The Cobras destroyed the recoilless rifle and stabilized the situation around the runway.

By this time, the two organized PRA counterattacks against the Navy SEALs around St George's were well underway. The first blow fell against Lt Erskine's 12-man team at the Radio Free Grenada station, now filled with wounded Grenadian militiamen from the standoff at 0900hrs. Little did Erskine and his men know that the PRA leadership at Fort Frederick had

One of the bloodiest confrontations of the entire campaign for the Rangers came when Grenadian army and militia units ambushed a machine-gun jeep crew, like the one above, that had taken a wrong turn at a junction to the northeast of Point Salines Airport, resulting in the deaths of four Rangers. (National Archives)

already directed Lt Cecil Prime, a loyal member of the RMC clique who was in charge of the antiaircraft defenses around St George's that had already inflicted serious harm on the incoming special forces units, to mount an assault to recapture the station. Prime took a platoon of PRA soldiers and a mortar crew in a BTR-60 APC and several civilian vehicles north from the capital toward Beauséjour, leaving Lt Nelson with the remainder of the Motorised and Mobile Companies near St George's. Arriving on scene at 0930hrs, Prime halted his assault force on a ridge several hundred yards to the south of the radio station to stage his attack. While the mortar crew provided covering fire, the APC advanced on the road toward the station from the southeast, while the platoon of soldiers advanced on foot through fields from the southwest in a pincer movement.

The SEALs spotted the imminent attack from their defensive perimeter, calling Erskine down from the roof of the station, where he was unsuccessfully trying to operate his radio. By the time he ordered his men to retreat to positions inside the main building, the mortars and the APC's heavy machine gun were pounding the station and beginning to obliterate its cinderblock walls. One SEAL, climbing back to the rooftop, gave his team a brief window to make their escape when he jammed the APC's gun turret with an RPG launched from his rifle. Erskine ordered his men to evacuate the radio station and follow a pre-planned line of retreat to the coastline. But before they could reach cover, they had to cross the large open meadow ringed by a chain-link fence topped with barbed wire that they had used as a landing zone several hours earlier. By this time, the advancing Grenadian soldiers were firing on them as the commandos fled across the field in leapfrog fashion, with one squad running about 30 yards while the second squad provided covering fire before switching roles. Three SEALs were wounded by bullets in the dash –

including Erskine, who was hit once in his canteen and a second time in his boot heel before a round shattered his elbow.

The Grenadians took several casualties of their own, and their cautiousness in pursuing the retreating SEALs allowed the commandos to cut through the fence with wire cutters and escape into the dense vegetation separating the meadow from Beauséjour Bay. In this small jungle, the SEALs waded across a neck-deep and fast-flowing river before reaching the coastline. There, they swam parallel to the beach to cover their tracks, then took refuge in the brush along the steep cliffs ringing the bay. Prime's soldiers pressed their search for the commandos all afternoon, coming as close as 10ft from the SEALs' hiding places in the jungle growth. The Grenadians called off their search at dusk, shortly before a Navy A-7 Corsair jet strafed the area and nearly hit the concealed SEALs. At this point, the commandos continued their escape by swimming out to sea, where Navy ships in the *Independence* carrier battle group recovered them by 0135hrs the next morning.

While Prime's assault was successfully driving Erskine's SEALs from the radio station, the PRA launched a larger counterattack to the south against Lt Leonard's 22-man team of Navy SEALs protecting Governor-General Scoon at Government House. The exchange of fire around the mansion ebbed and flowed in the early part of the morning as the SEALs defending the grounds kept watch on their surroundings. At one point, three soldiers armed with AK-47s approached the house along its U-shaped driveway. When the concealed SEALs called for them to halt, the soldiers instead leveled their rifles, triggering an immediate cascade of fire from the waiting commandos. The SEALs' bullets cut down at least one of the Grenadians and dispersed or killed the rest.

Meanwhile, Grenada's military leaders at Fort Frederick were organizing a substantial force to recapture Government House and its occupants. Lt Col. Ewart Layne, Austin's deputy both on the governing council and

Attempting to cover the escape of the Navy SEALs, USS Caron fires on the Radio Free Grenada station from its position in Beauséjour Bay. Navy Corsair jets strafing the area nearly hit the SEALs before they could swim out to the safety of the ships offshore. (Mike Leahy, Navy Art Collection, Naval History and Heritage Command)

THE NAVY SEAL MISSION TO RESCUE GOVERNOR-GENERAL SCOON AT GOVERNMENT HOUSE, 1015HRS, OCTOBER 25, 1983 (PP.56–57)

US special forces launched three clandestine missions on the morning of October 25 to protect Grenadians who would restore democracy in the campaign's aftermath. The most critical of these missions was the rescue of Governor-General Sir Paul Scoon from house arrest in his official residence, Government House.

A 22-man detachment from Navy SEAL Team 6, led by Lt Wellington "Duke" Leonard, arrived at Government House around 0630hrs in two UH-60 Black Hawks. Heavy ground fire drove off the helicopters before the overall SEAL commander, Capt. Robert Gormly, could land. The SEALs quickly secured Scoon inside the mansion and took up defensive positions around the grounds and on Government House's balconies (1), but their planned rapid extraction was not possible.

Recognizing the SEALs' vulnerability, the Grenadian military command ordered a counterattack against Government House. At 1000hrs, the pincer attack began, intending to trap the isolated SEALs between PRA infantry advancing on the mansion from the northwest (2) and a strong detachment of infantry and a BTR-60 APC from the PRA Motorised Company advancing along the road to the southeast (3).

Leonard ordered his outnumbered force, armed with only rifles and pistols, to hold their fire for as long as possible while he attempted to call in air support using a handheld radio. As the firefight escalated, Leonard was finally able to connect with Gormly at Point Salines, who relayed his situation to an Air Force Spectre gunship nearby. Just as the Grenadian APC crashed through the gates, rumbled up the driveway toward Government House, and began to open fire with its powerful guns, the Spectre arrived over the scene and unleashed its cannons, destroying the APC and blunting the attack (4). A second Spectre drove back the PRA soldiers advancing on the mansion from the northwest.

The Grenadian forces regrouped and renewed their pincer attack with additional APCs throughout the afternoon and evening of October 25, which the SEALs repelled each time with the indispensable aid of Spectre gunships. They maintained their positions at Government House until Marines arrived to relieve them early the following morning.

in command of the PRA, directed the attack, though he likely remained in Fort Frederick rather than overseeing the assault in person as Prime had done at the radio station. Layne ordered a pincer attack on the mansion to overwhelm its isolated defenders: while a force of infantry from the PRA security platoon stationed on Mount Wheldale advanced on Government House from the northwest, an additional force anchored around an APC with supporting infantry drawn from Nelson's Motorised Company would breach the mansion's gates from the road to the southeast, trapping the Americans between them. The Navy SEALs, for their part, were lightly armed with only rifles and pistols, with no heavy weapons to counter armored vehicles.

At around 1000hrs, the SEALs spotted Grenadian infantry approaching on foot from the northwest through the wooded area and across the tennis court that separated Government House from the official residences of Coard and the deceased Bishop. Meanwhile, an APC rumbled down the road from the southeast, halting outside the mansion's gate. Lt Leonard, knowing his team was outmanned and outgunned, ordered his men to delay their fire for as long as possible to conceal from the Grenadians their defensive positions and the limited extent of their firepower. Realizing his team could not hold off the armored attack on their own, he desperately tried to call in air support. However, with access to only a handheld radio with limited range and battery life, he was unable to make direct contact with Air Force planes nearby. He opted instead to contact Capt. Gormly at the special forces command post at Point Salines, and Gormly was able to relay Leonard's request to an Air Force Spectre gunship flying offshore.

The Grenadian counterattacks on October 25 were anchored around the seven BTR-60 APCs of the PRA's elite Motorised Company. These Soviet-built vehicles brought the heavy firepower of their machine guns to bear against the lightly armed Navy SEALs at Government House and Radio Free Grenada. (National Archives)

The heavily armed Spectre arrived over Government House just as the APC crashed through the front gate and began to advance up the driveway and open fire with its powerful machine gun. As the APC swung its gun turret toward the mansion, the side-mounted cannons of the Spectre hit the armored vehicle squarely and reduced it to rubble. A second Spectre quickly joined the fray and repulsed the infantry advancing on the mansion from the opposite direction. By 1015hrs, the two Spectre gunships had driven back the Grenadian attack in the nick of time.

But the danger to Government House was not yet over. The Spectres remained circling overhead until they had to fly off to refuel at their bases in Barbados and Puerto Rico around noon. As fighting waxed and waned from the direction of the nearby residences on Mount Wheldale, Scoon and his wife continued to hunker on the floor of their dining room shelter, able to rest on a mahogany couch only during brief lulls in the shooting. "As the sounds of gunfire resounded in our ears," Scoon recalled, "the portraits of members of the Royal Family – past and present – looked down solemnly upon us as we quietly and humbly lay on the bare hard wooden floor."

By mid-afternoon, Layne's PRA force had regrouped sufficiently to make another assault to recapture the governor-general's house. Now reinforced with two more APCs from Nelson's Motorised Company on the road approaching from the southeast, a Grenadian force of 30 soldiers advanced again from the vicinity of Bishop's former residence to renew their pincer attack on Government House around 1530hrs. Most of the SEALs were positioned in a defensive perimeter around the outside of the mansion and prepared to meet the onslaught with their rifles and pistols. By this time, Leonard's handheld radio batteries were running low and he could no longer make consistent contact with Gormly at Point Salines to request air support. Improvising, Leonard picked up the landline phone in Scoon's dining room. Connecting with an operator, he used his long-distance calling card to place a call to the United States. Transferred from JSOC headquarters at Fort Bragg in North Carolina to the Air Force operations center at Hurlburt Field in Florida, Leonard was eventually patched through via radio to the pilot of one of the Spectre gunships over Grenada. Leonard, now communicating directly with the Spectre pilot, provided the necessary coordinates and clearances for the gunship to zero in. The pilot unleashed his aircraft's cannons on the armored vehicles, disabling one and forcing the second to withdraw. Then it strafed the wooded area behind the mansion where Grenadian soldiers were advancing on foot, sending those who were not killed into headlong retreat beyond their staging area near the empty prime minister's residence, which the Spectre set ablaze with more fire.

The repulse of this second major attack gave the besieged SEALs a longer reprieve – but only for a time. Spectre gunships remained circling protectively overhead for most of the afternoon, with occasional breaks to refuel. But scattered PRA soldiers kept up a nagging fire on Government House to keep the weary defenders, now running perilously low on ammunition, on edge.

One final major attack came in the evening after sundown around 2000hrs. Once again, an APC rumbled toward the mansion from the road to the southeast while a group of 15–20 Grenadian soldiers massed for an assault across the ground to the northwest. With no Spectre gunships in the immediate vicinity, Adm. Metcalf considered using naval gunfire from the fleet offshore to support the SEALs as the firefight escalated into a

The Air Force's heavily armed AC-130 Spectre gunships provided vital air support throughout the Grenada campaign, proving particularly indispensable in driving back the repeated PRA armored counterattacks against the Navy SEALs at Government House. (Attilio Sinagra, USAF Art Collection, National Archives)

full-fledged battle. But he rejected this option for fear that the naval artillery would inflict as much harm on the commandos as on their attackers. The desperation of the situation was palpable on the deck of Metcalf's flagship, USS *Guam*, where radios picked up sporadic calls from the SEALs that one Navy officer recalled "made it appear that they were in the last few minutes of the Alamo."

Finally, at 2215hrs, a Spectre arrived on scene and drove back the attack, remaining overhead to protect the SEALs and the governor-general into the night. The major Grenadian attacks against Government House had ended, but the American outpost on Mount Wheldale remained isolated and under siege deep behind enemy lines. Scoon later recalled that, for himself as well as the SEALs, "there was no sleep during the long and perilous night that followed the dismal and dreadful day."

The fulcrum: The Americans strike back

Well before these final attacks on Government House, the American commanders at Point Salines and aboard USS *Guam* were searching in vain for a way to relieve the pressure on the besieged Navy SEALs. The situation at Government House seemed even more desperate in the fog of war than it was in reality, as early reports indicated that the SEALs had sustained heavy casualties and were running low on ammunition. Seeking to break the deadlock and support the SEALs, Adm. Metcalf made the fateful decision to make a series of improvised changes to the preexisting invasion plans. These improvisations initially met with disaster, bringing about the nadir of American battlefield fortunes in Operation *Urgent Fury* when the already-fraying plans for the US-led mission seemed to be coming apart at the seams. But this period of maximum peril for American forces proved to be the fulcrum moment of the battle, as Metcalf's response to the setbacks decisively swung the tide of the campaign in the Americans' favor.

Following the first Grenadian counterattack against Government House in the mid-morning of October 25, Gormly and Scholtes appealed to Metcalf to send ground forces to relieve the surrounded SEALs. Metcalf had no firsthand view of the situation around St George's from his perch on the bridge of the *Guam* positioned off the coast from Pearls on the opposite side of the island. Moreover, he had not been briefed on the details of the special operations missions that had been formed at the Pentagon without his participation, but he soon learned of the "paramount importance" of the rescue of Governor-General Scoon.

Around noon, Metcalf consulted with his Army advisor, Maj. Gen. Norman Schwarzkopf, on ways to provide direct assistance to the imperiled missions around the capital city. Knowing that the Rangers were fully engaged at Point Salines and unlikely to reach St George's anytime soon, the two commanders sought out other options to relieve pressure on the SEALs. Schwarzkopf proposed a daring plan to open a second front against the Grenadian and Cuban forces on the western side of the island by landing Marines north of St George's to advance on the capital and link up with the embattled SEALs. One company of Marines, still aboard its amphibious transports offshore, would land by sea while helicopters ferried a second company by air across the island from Pearls. The plan carried the significant risk of landing the invasion's only reserve force on an unscouted beach against an enemy force of unknown strength. But this envelopment maneuver stood the best chance of overwhelming the Grenadian forces that threatened to overtake the vulnerable American positions around the capital.

However, this major amphibious undertaking could not take place for a number of hours as the *Guam* and its support ships carrying Marines circled the island to take up positions off Grenada's west coast. In the meantime, Metcalf made another bold decision to aid the SEALs. Ruling out bombardment from Navy ships or aircraft as too likely to inflict collateral damage on civilian buildings in St George's, the admiral ordered Marine Cobra helicopters to attack Fort Frederick. Metcalf reasoned that the precise fire of the Cobras offered the best chance of striking back against the Grenadian military command post that was directing the counterattacks against the SEALs – and whose antiaircraft guns had wreaked havoc on the Black Hawks carrying the Delta Force operators to Richmond Hill Prison.

Shortly after 1300hrs, two Sea Cobra gunship helicopters arrived over St George's to mount their attack on Fort Frederick. The pilots of the two helicopters, Capt. Timothy Howard and Capt. John "Pat" Giguere, coordinated their attack so that one would make a pass at their target while the other distracted its defenders. Over the course of five passes, the Cobras hurled fire down on Fort Frederick from their side-mounted rockets and Gatling gun-style cannons under the helicopters' noses. But on the fifth pass, at 1327hrs, several rounds of antiaircraft fire tore through Howard's chopper, destroying both of its engines and knocking unconscious his co-pilot, Capt. Jeb Seagle.

Howard, himself critically wounded by rounds that broke his leg and nearly severed his arm, struggled to direct his helicopter into a controlled crash in a sports field on the outskirts of St George's. The crash, which broke off the tail rotor, jolted Seagle back to consciousness, and the co-pilot pulled Howard from the flaming wreckage into overgrowth on the side of the field. Grenadian soldiers from the nearby garrison advanced on the smoking

The Marines put their heavily armed attack helicopters, AH-1T Sea Cobra gunships, to use in every sector of the fighting on Grenada, but the downing of the two Cobras that attacked Fort Frederick marked the low point of US military fortunes in the operation. (National Archives)

wreck site and fired their AK-47s at the downed pilots. Howard sent Seagle off to find help, while Giguere's Cobra circled back to repel the advancing Grenadians and protect Howard. By this time, unbeknownst to Howard or Giguere, Seagle had been killed by Grenadian pursuers on his flight toward St George's to retrieve help.

Within minutes, a rescue helicopter – flying just 10ft above the water's surface – evaded the antiaircraft guns around the harbor and landed near the crash site while Giguere's Cobra provided covering fire against Grenadian antiaircraft guns and ground soldiers in the area. The double-rotor Sea Knight recovered the gravely injured Howard and made its escape out of the harbor while Giguere once again sought to protect it from Grenadian

Capt. Jeb Seagle pulls pilot Capt. Timothy Howard from the burning wreck of their downed Cobra helicopter. While Seagle went in search of help, the explosion of the helicopter sent ignited rockets in all directions like fireworks, deterring Grenadian soldiers from approaching the crash site before Howard could be rescued. (Mike Leahy, Navy Art Collection, Naval History and Heritage Command)

attack. Giguere focused his efforts against the antiaircraft guns positioned on the southern edge of the harbor's mouth near the government headquarters at Butler House, since American airstrikes had taken the guns to the north at Fort Rupert out of action earlier in the day. He used his guns and rockets to strafe the antiaircraft position. Just as the rescue helicopter safely left St George's Harbour at 1340hrs, its pilots spotted Giguere's Cobra – apparently out of ammunition – seeking to deter the Grenadian guns simply with its imposing presence. But as it turned to follow the Sea Knight to safety, the Cobra was shot down and crashed into the sea just outside the mouth of the harbor, killing Giguere and his co-pilot.

Though the rescue helicopter completed its successful escape and evacuation of Howard, whose life was saved, the loss of the two Cobras and three pilots for little tangible military benefit marked the low point of the campaign for Metcalf and his American forces. This disaster magnified the sense on the deck of the *Guam* that the mission had run off the rails: the SEALs remained imperiled at Government House, while the Grenadians had driven back the SEALs from the radio station and Delta Force from the prison; meanwhile, the Rangers were stalled at Point Salines after discovering that most of the American students remained behind enemy lines. Now two Cobras had been lost.

Seeking a decisive way to turn the tables, Metcalf reconsidered the use of Navy aircraft to bomb the Grenadian military headquarters despite the risk of collateral damage. Asking Schwarzkopf for his views, the Army general unequivocally advised, "Bomb it." Knowing of the central role the fort had played in organizing the morning's counterattacks, he told Metcalf, "If we let them keep up an organized resistance, we'll take a lot more casualties and eventually have to bomb it anyhow." Metcalf unleashed Navy Corsair jets from USS *Independence* at 1345hrs, just five minutes after the crash of Giguere's Cobra, to launch an airstrike on Fort Frederick and other fortified Grenadian positions around St George's. The attack destroyed Grenada's military command center and virtually ended the centralized direction of Grenadian resistance. "In hindsight, the battle was won right there," Metcalf later wrote. "From that time on, everything was local action." Radio traffic out of Fort Frederick ceased.

Metcalf may have overstated the definitive impact of the airstrike on Fort Frederick, but only marginally so. The thick stone walls of the colonial fortress protected the PRA high command in its underground bunker from physical harm, but in a psychological sense the attack was even more effective. With their communications disrupted and the full

Capt. Pat Giguere's Cobra gunship, hit by antiaircraft fire while covering the escape of the rescue helicopter carrying the wounded Capt. Howard, plunges into the sea just outside St George's Harbour. The double-rotor Sea Knight rescue helicopter is visible escaping to safety on the right. (Associated Press/Alamy)

The colonial-era stone fortress Fort Frederick was the Grenadian military command center and the headquarters for the RMC regime during the campaign. Its antiaircraft guns shot down two US helicopters from their perch atop a high ridge east of St George's before an American airstrike destroyed the guns and command post. (David Stanley from Nanaimo, Canada, CC BY 2.0 https://creativecommons.org/licenses/by/2.0, via Wikimedia Commons)

extent of American firepower on display, Gen. Austin, Lt Col. Layne, and their RMC colleagues played little further documented role in the battle, though they remained hunkered in place for the rest of the day. American commanders later learned that the airstrike had also inflicted the toll on Grenadian civilians that Metcalf had sought to avoid: one bomb hit the unmarked civilian mental hospital at Fort Matthew next to Fort Frederick, killing 21 patients and releasing others into the streets of St George's.

Crisis and reinforcement at Point Salines

The afternoon began well for the Rangers at Point Salines. With the runway and the high ground to the north secure, the Cuban Old Camp captured, and the students at True Blue campus in safety, the Rangers accelerated their push toward Little Havana. By 1100hrs, Rangers from the 1st Battalion secured Point Salines Airport's fuel storage tanks north of the terminal and began to surround Little Havana. This newer compound was located just over a mile to the northeast of the terminal, fenced off in a depression surrounded by hills on three sides, where Cuban construction workers – including those who had fled from the Old Camp – manned hastily constructed defensive positions. The compound itself included barracks buildings still under construction as well as the Cuban mission, where Col. Pedro Tortoló Comas and the Cuban military advisors who had been pulled from their posts with the PRA established their headquarters. Ranger snipers kept the Cubans pinned down as they searched for any movement inside the compound, leaving 18 Cubans killed or wounded.

The Rangers initially planned to hold their positions and wait to assault Little Havana until the arrival of reinforcements from the 82nd Airborne Division, but an unexpected problem arose in the late morning that demanded faster action. Two Rangers from the 2nd Battalion, who landed on the runway with the follow-on waves of troops, took off on motorcycles to join the fray north of the airport, but Cuban defenders shot them down as they approached Little Havana, leaving the wounded soldiers stranded in no-man's land between American and Cuban lines. Around 1400hrs, improvising a plan to neutralize the compound more rapidly, the Rangers used a bullhorn to issue an ultimatum to the defenders, demanding that the Cubans in Little Havana surrender or face attack. The blunt message prompted about 175 Cubans to surrender, leaving just 80–100 holdouts in the compound for a later cleanup mission. Although Tortoló and his dwindling assembly of officers and construction workers remained, this second en masse Cuban surrender effectively ended large-scale organized Cuban resistance on Grenada.

By this time, the Rangers had assistance in keeping watch over their growing body of prisoners. At 1045hrs, the first units of the Caribbean Peacekeeping Force, commanded by Brig. Rudyard Lewis, landed at Point Salines Airport from Barbados. No one on the ground, including Lewis, had been briefed on the role that Caribbean forces would take in the ongoing ground operations, but the 353 soldiers and policemen from the Caribbean coalition were eager to play a part in the mission. Lewis and his American counterparts assigned the Caribbean forces to guard the Cuban and Grenadian prisoners on the airport grounds and in the former Cuban Old Camp just to the north, which they transformed into a detention facility.

No sooner had the Rangers precipitated the surrender of the bulk of Cuban forces in Little Havana than the first planeload of paratroopers from the 82nd Airborne Division landed on the runway of Point Salines Airport at 1405hrs. Among them was Maj. Gen. Edward Trobaugh, the commander of the division and what would be designated Task Force 121 for Operation *Urgent Fury*. Plans for the operation called for the 82nd Airborne to assume occupation and peacekeeping duties from the Rangers once combat operations had concluded before the end of the first day. Instead, these two Army forces would fight side-by-side for the next two days.

Trobaugh was alarmed at the situation that welcomed him at Point Salines. Sporadic but significant gunfire still zipped past the paratroopers who disembarked from the large Air Force C-141 Starlifter transport planes that

When two Rangers riding motorcycles toward the fighting north of Point Salines were shot down and stranded in no-man's land between American and Cuban lines, the Rangers improvised a rescue plan that triggered the surrender of most of the remaining Cubans in Little Havana. (National Archives)

carried them and their supplies from Fort Bragg in the US. After conferring with Rangers' 1st Battalion commander Lt Col. Taylor at his command post at the edge of the runway, Trobaugh made his way to the airport terminal at 1530hrs to meet with Scholtes, who brought him up to speed on the situation on the ground. Trobaugh outranked both Scholtes and Schwarzkopf, making him the senior Army commander in the field. For the time being, however, he and Scholtes agreed to temporarily set up separate headquarters and split command duties of the ground forces, leaving the Rangers and special forces to the JSOC commander.

At around the same time as this commanders' conference in the airport terminal, the far end of the runway came under attack. The PRA was able to organize one final counterattack against US forces, this time against the heart of the American position at Point Salines. The Grenadian attack on the northeastern perimeter of Point Salines Airport was a desperate gamble launched with three armored vehicles carrying 24 PRA soldiers from the elite Motorised Company under Lt Nelson. Though the assault would use the PRA's last three APCs, Nelson himself did not lead the attack, thinking it too weak and isolated to be anything more than futile. The APC platoon chief in the lead vehicle had little sense of the position or strength of the forces he would confront. At best, the attack would reclaim control of the eastern end of the runway, and at the least the Grenadians hoped to disable an American aircraft on the runway to shut down the airport.

Fortunately for the Americans, a patrol of Rangers searching for survivors of the morning jeep ambush spotted the rapidly approaching armored vehicles and radioed a warning to the main Ranger force in the hills north of the runway. The Ranger patrol fired on the APC column as it passed to no effect, but the Grenadians had lost the crucial element of surprise. As the APCs stormed toward the runway, firing their turret machine guns in all directions, the waiting Rangers met them with fire from rifles, machine guns, mortars, and shoulder-mounted antitank weapons, several of which struck the lead vehicle. The APC screeched to a halt and reversed course, only to collide with the second APC. Further hits from rockets disabled the vehicles and the crews bailed out, leaving two dead and taking more casualties as they retreated. The third APC sought to turn around and escape, but by this time a Spectre gunship had zeroed in, destroying it with a blast of firepower that flipped it over off the road.

The attack had the potential to significantly disrupt American operations at Point Salines, but it came too late in the day and was too weak to have any real chance of success. Had it come earlier in the day, around the time of the counterattacks against the SEALs and before the Rangers had consolidated their position around Point Salines, it might have significantly impacted the course of the campaign. Instead, the PRA command committed its main attack force, Nelson's combined Motorised and Mobile Companies, in a piecemeal fashion that diluted its power. By the time of the APC attack on the airport, the PRA was no longer strong enough to significantly damage the invading forces.

However, the PRA was still able to inflict pain on the Americans. As the Ranger patrol that had first spotted the approaching APCs continued with its mission on the roads northeast of the airport, it came under ambush from a group of Grenadian soldiers who had escaped the failed APC attack, perhaps supplemented with forces from Capt. Redhead's security platoons stationed

The Grenadian armored counterattack on Point Salines was a desperate gamble that resulted in the destruction of the PRA's three remaining APCs, including one knocked out by fire from a Spectre gunship. The attack was likely mounted at the urging of Cuban officials, making it the only documented military action coordinated between Grenadian and Cuban forces. (National Archives)

nearby. An extended firefight raged for about 90 minutes while a Ranger lieutenant lay seriously wounded from the initial exchange of fire. Finally, Navy air support from USS *Independence* bombed the Grenadian positions and brought the fight to an end, leveling the large house of an RMC official in which the PRA soldiers were taking shelter.

The APC counterattack and the subsequent ambush alarmed Trobaugh enough to request reinforcements from units of the 82nd Airborne still in the US. Against the advice of Schwarzkopf on the *Guam* offshore, Trobaugh called back to Fort Bragg and issued the order to "send me battalions until I tell you to stop." Metcalf granted him temporary command of the two battalions of Rangers around Point Salines at 1900hrs, though the Ranger commanders themselves did not learn this news until the following morning. As the fighting around the airport waned by the late afternoon, the American commanders did not yet realize that the counterattack against the runway was the last gasp of organized Grenadian resistance.

Marine landing at Grand Mal

As darkness fell over the war-torn island, the Marines were finally in position to mount their amphibious landing on the west coast north of St George's. Grand Mal Bay had been hastily scouted by Lt Michael Walsh's Navy SEAL Team 4 as a suitable landing zone. But the beach at Grand Mal was far from ideal, arcing in a long crescent with high ground rising steeply beyond an exceptionally narrow beach. In addition, a complex of fuel storage tanks stood at one end of the landing zone, a highly flammable barrier that marked one of the main exit routes from the beach.

Despite these hazards – and mistaken fears that one or more battalions of Cuban soldiers were stationed in the vicinity – the Marines launched their amphibious operation and landed unopposed on the beach at Grand Mal Bay at 1900hrs. One company established a secure perimeter around the beachhead and cleared a landing zone for the helicopters that would carry the second company of Marines across the island from Pearls and Grenville. Though the Marine landing at Grand Mal was unfolding successfully,

Metcalf and his fellow commanders on the *Guam* feared that they would reach Government House too late to rescue the embattled SEALs and Governor-General Scoon.

By nightfall of the first day's fighting, the tide of the battle had turned decisively in the Americans' favor. The successive blows in the afternoon of the bombing of PRA headquarters at Fort Frederick, the surrender of most of the Cuban force, the failure of the Grenadian counterattack at Point Salines, and the landing of the Marines at Grand Mal Bay marked the key ingredients of the turning point of the battle. The fight was not yet over, but the end was far closer than US forces realized.

DAY 2: TO THE RESCUE

The second day of combat in Grenada focused on two critical rescue missions: of the besieged Navy SEALs protecting Governor-General Sir Paul Scoon at Government House, who endured significant attacks from Grenadian forces into the night of October 25; and of the American medical students at the main campus of St George's Medical School, located south of the capital at Grand Anse. These operations took place in the context of the steady crumbling of organized resistance from Grenadian and Cuban forces around St George's and Point Salines, and their successful accomplishment marked the de facto end of the battle for control of Grenada's strategic points.

Marines advance, resistance dissolves

By the predawn hours of October 26, the Marines had begun their advance on the capital city. The force was now two companies strong after the overnight helicopter transit of units from Pearls Airport, complete with jeeps, 13 amtracs, and five tanks. The Marine ground commander, Lt Col. Ray Smith, had also arrived in the early-morning hours at Grand Mal Bay, from where his troops began their advance south along the narrow roads toward St George's. The Marines reached the Queen's Park Racetrack on the northern outskirts of the capital by 0430hrs after encountering minimal resistance, prompting Smith to send a detachment of about 60 Marines to rapidly make the trek up Mount Wheldale to assess the situation around Government House.

The landing of the Marine force at Grand Mal and its armored advance on St George's completed the rout of Grenadian forces in the area without having to employ its firepower. The PRA command, in its last effort to put up a roadblock against the invaders, had ordered the final remnants of Lt Nelson's depleted force to take up positions along the northern approaches to the capital from Grand Mal. But these soldiers, upon hearing the menacing rumble of Marine tanks rolling toward them, opted to drop their guns, shed their uniforms, and melt into the civilian populace rather than stage a last stand. The Grenadian military leadership came to the same conclusion. Before the sun rose over Fort Frederick, Gen. Austin, Bernard Coard, and the rest of the RMC leaders agreed that the situation was hopeless and fled their command post in civilian clothing to go into hiding.

The first Marine units arrived on Mount Wheldale at 0600hrs to find the area virtually deserted of Grenadian troops, who had also fled during the night and left behind trucks filled with arms and equipment near their staging

N

Calivigny
Military Compound

Fort Frederick

Richmond Hill
Prison

Mount Wheldale (Government House)

Gormly

Team 6 SEAL

Queen's Park Racetrack

22 MAU Faulkner/Smith

① St George's

Fort Rupert

Grand Anse Medical School Campus ④

PRA/PRM ③

Grand Anse Beach

TG 20.5 Berry

TF 124 Erie

XXX JTF 120 Metcalf

⑤

True Blue Medical School Campus

Frequente

Tortoló

Cuban Force ② 2/82 Silvasy
Calliste

82 Trobaugh

TF 121 Trobaugh

TF 123 SOF

Scholes
Airport Terminal

1/75 Taylor

CPF Lewis

2/75 Hagler

Point Salines

1. At 0430hrs, Marines advance from Grand Mal Bay to the Queen's Park Racetrack north of St George's, then to Government House, relieving the SEALs by 0600hrs and bringing Scoon to safety. By 1700hrs, they enter Fort Frederick unopposed.
2. At 0630hrs, the 2nd Brigade of the 82nd Airborne Division attacks Little Havana, capturing it by 0835hrs.
3. After capturing the PRA supply depot at Frequente at 1400hrs, a platoon of the 82nd Airborne repels an ambush from Grenadian or Cuban forces to the east.
4. At 1605hrs, the Army, Navy, Marines, and Air Force bombard the area around Grand Anse with artillery and airpower to precede the Ranger rescue mission.
5. At 1615hrs, the 2nd Ranger Battalion leads a helicopter rescue mission from the Point Salines Airport to evacuate students from the Grand Anse medical school campus.

0   1km
0   1 mile

area at Bishop's former home. The Marines made contact with the SEALs, who were still imperturbably manning their posts on the grounds of Government House, and secured the area by 0710hrs. Lt Col. Smith, who had established his command post at Queen's Park, was astonished to receive the news that none of the SEALs or members of Scoon's party had been killed or seriously wounded.

Lt Duke Leonard and his SEAL team continued their protective watch over the governor-general, who quickly gathered some essentials with his wife in preparation to leave their home and refuge for the past 24 hours. The Marines and SEALs insisted that Scoon and his party travel by foot along backroads to Queen's Park rather than risk a helicopter extraction directly from Government House, as they were still unsure of the level of resistance that lingered in the area. Indeed, Scoon reported coming under scattered fire at one point as they passed the detritus of the previous day's battle, which caused him to slip and fall. Once safely at Queen's Park, Scoon and his wife were flown by helicopter to USS *Guam* at 0857hrs to rest, refit, and

The Marine landing at Grand Mal Bay and advance on St George's with tanks and amtracs convinced both the Grenadian military leadership and the soldiers and militia on the ground that further organized resistance against US forces was fruitless. (Mike Leahy, Art Collection, National Museum of the Marine Corps)

meet with Adm. Metcalf over tea and a hearty breakfast. The American commander reported with relief to his superiors in Washington that the rescue of the governor-general of Grenada, so critical to the political success of the operation, was at last complete.

Scoon insisted that he return to the island to join his countrymen in the early afternoon, traveling by helicopter to Point Salines. The governor-general made his way to the headquarters of the Caribbean forces at the Great House, where he signed back-dated letters officially requesting military intervention from the OECS, Barbados, Jamaica, and the US. Ever conscious of upholding the proprieties of his office in carrying out his duties, Scoon declined to make any broadcasts or decisions about the future of Grenada's government until after the end of hostilities.

Meanwhile, around noon, the Marines continued their advance from Government House on Mount Wheldale along the eastern edge of St George's toward Fort Frederick, proceeding cautiously as they kept a vigilant watch for the Grenadian and Cuban battalions rumored to be nearby. But all they found were two empty and abandoned armored scout cars from the PRA Motorised Company, so they quickened their pace. A group of about ten Grenadians was descending the walls of Fort Frederick as the Marines approached, shedding their uniforms as they fled. The Marines encountered no resistance when they entered the fort at 1700hrs. They found the Grenadian military command center deserted and discovered large stores of Soviet-made weapons and ammunition, official documents of Grenada's military relationship with the Soviet Union and Cuba, and maps of Grenadian military defenses across the island.

This discovery, coupled with other ammunition stores uncovered across Grenada, served a political purpose as well as a military one, helping the US-led coalition justify the necessity of the intervention to a skeptical international community.

Last gasp of Cuban resistance

Gen. Trobaugh's 82nd Airborne Division was prepared to enter the fray by the morning of October 26. The last of Trobaugh's initial wave of troops and supplies, two battalions strong from the 2nd Brigade under Col. Stephen Silvasy, had finally completed its landing at Point Salines at 0245hrs, replacing the Rangers in their positions on the hills surrounding Little Havana. Trobaugh planned to launch an assault soon after daybreak to capture the Cuban headquarters compound and the 80–100 holdouts who remained entrenched there. Though few in number, the surrounded Cubans had received stark orders from Fidel Castro overnight to fight to the last man.

Before dawn had broken, several officers from the company that would lead the assault, from the 2nd Battalion of the 325th Infantry under Lt Col. Jack Hamilton, ventured beyond American lines to scout the hills overlooking Little Havana from the west. They stumbled upon a Cuban outpost and a firefight broke out that killed the American company commander. The exchange of fire grew more intense when a platoon of paratroopers advanced to support their wounded officers. Using captured AK-47s and Soviet-made hand grenades to supplement their diminished ammunition, the paratroopers drove the Cubans from the hill.

The full assault on Little Havana began at 0630hrs, as Hamilton's battalion advanced on the Cubans' positions through significant fire that

The Americans dubbed the Cuban headquarters compound "Little Havana." Located near the village of Calliste north of Point Salines, the camp was still under construction and was poorly situated for defense, with high ground surrounding it on three sides. (National Archives)

wounded several paratroopers. Hamilton called in support for his attack from Army artillery and Navy Corsair jets. The Navy jets in particular inflicted numerous casualties on the Cubans as they made four strafing and bombing runs that pummeled the compound's cinderblock buildings. Finally, the Cubans who had retreated to their central headquarters building replaced their large Cuban flag with white sheets to signal their surrender. The Americans took over 80 Cuban prisoners, including 29 wounded, and 16 Cubans died in the attack. Only three Cubans, including Col. Tortoló, managed to escape to the Soviet embassy near Grand Anse. The paratroopers declared Little Havana secure by 0835hrs, though one additional paratrooper was killed soon after the attack when a Cuban artillery gun that he was trying to disable exploded.

The 82nd Airborne paratroopers continued their advance beyond the Cuban compound toward the village of Frequente to the east, the site of the Grenadian antiaircraft guns that had fired on the parachuting Rangers the day before. They found the PRA's main supply depot there at 1400hrs, capturing a vast store of weapons, ammunition, and vehicles from the lone guard on duty, adding to the propaganda boost that supported American claims of the militant intentions of Grenada's socialist regime. Suffering in the tropical heat, the battalion took up defensive positions on a ridge to the north of the logistics base.

At about the same time, a platoon of six jeeps from Hamilton's paratrooper battalion, which had been sent to recover the bodies of the ambushed Ranger jeep crew from the previous day, came under ambush themselves near a drive-in movie theater to the east of Frequente. Using the machine guns mounted on their jeeps, the paratroopers repelled the attack without suffering any casualties while inflicting four deaths on their ambushers and destroying an armored scout car. The firefight turned out to be the last substantial attack from Grenadian or Cuban forces (their identity was unconfirmed) on the Point Salines peninsula.

Rescuing the students at Grand Anse

The overriding focus for the American commanders on the second day of the campaign was the rescue of the American medical students at the main campus of St George's Medical School, situated on Grand Anse Bay along one of the most picturesque beaches in the Caribbean. Adm. Metcalf was coming under increasing pressure from officials in Washington to evacuate the remaining students as quickly as possible, but he was not satisfied with the initial plans to accomplish the mission. Gen. Trobaugh, now in sole command of the ground forces around Point Salines after the departure of Gen. Scholtes following the recovery of his Navy SEAL team from Government House, proposed to advance toward Grand Anse by land. He insisted that the rough terrain and intelligence reports of a large enemy force blocking the route would delay his arrival at the campus for at least another 24 hours.

The commanders aboard USS *Guam*, now positioned directly offshore from the Grand Anse campus, sought alternative means to reach the students more rapidly. Gen. Schwarzkopf, gazing from the bridge of the *Guam* toward shore, devised a joint-service plan to use the tools they had on hand to rescue the students in a matter of hours. He proposed using the Marine transport helicopters on the flight deck of the *Guam* – which had ferried the Marines to Pearls and Grand Mal the day before – to carry Army Rangers the short distance from Point Salines directly to the beach in front of the medical school campus to extract the students in a seaward direction rather than by land. Metcalf quickly approved the improvised plan, and Schwarzkopf overrode the objections of Marine commander Col. James Faulkner to begin preparations. As the Marine helicopters deployed to the Point Salines airfield, the commander of the Marine helicopter squadron, Lt Col. Granville Amos, hashed out the details of the operation with the Ranger commander who would lead the rescue, Lt Col. Ralph Hagler. The Rangers learned the layout of the buildings at Grand Anse from students who had been rescued from the True Blue campus, and they were able to communicate directly with the students at Grand Anse using radios and telephones to prepare them for what was to come.

The rescue mission launched at 1605hrs with a bombardment of suspected Grenadian positions around the Grand Anse campus from Army artillery, Navy Corsair jets, Marine Cobra helicopters, and Air Force Spectre gunships. The massive firepower set ablaze a former hotel building nearby and destroyed an antiaircraft gun, the only heavy weaponry that could threaten the approaching helicopters. Grenadian defenses in the area were oriented toward an expected approach of American forces by land from the south. The soldiers in the immediate vicinity of the campus, only 15–20 men strong, were mostly militiamen assigned to Lt Callistus Bernard's Exploration Company, which had hitherto played little role in the battle. These forces dispersed to take cover from the bombardment but remained in the area.

Vice Adm. Joseph Metcalf speaks with a group of Army Rangers at the Point Salines airfield before the mission to rescue the students from the Grand Anse medical school campus. The Rangers were given some of the most critical missions on all three days of combat. (National Archives)

The students had been instructed to gather in a dormitory building close to the beach, marking their position with white sheets and themselves with white armbands while propping mattresses against the windows for protection. Only seconds after the fearsome bombardment ceased at 1615hrs, the students witnessed a line of double-rotor CH-46 Sea Knight helicopters flying toward the beach. Nine helicopters in groups of three successively landed on the narrow, palm-tree-lined beach to deposit the Rangers from Hagler's 2nd Battalion. In all, 150 Rangers waded through the surf to establish a defensive perimeter around the campus while Hagler and Amos directed the operation from their command helicopter hovering offshore. The Sea Knights and the Rangers on the ground took scattered but significant fire from the AK-47s of the Grenadian defenders, and shrapnel from Grenadian mortars also posed a risk. But the greatest threat to the helicopters turned out to be the challenging landscape, as the rotors of two helicopters struck palm trees on the narrow beach, damaging one and disabling the other, forcing it to be abandoned.

Once the Rangers had landed, the Sea Knights departed to clear space for five heavy-lifting CH-53 Sea Stallions, the single-rotor helicopters that would ferry the students to safety. The Sea Stallions landed on the beach one at a time as the Rangers guided the students from their assembly area in the dorms across the beach and into the waiting choppers. Though sporadic gunfire continued to menace the area, none of the students were injured. The Rangers successfully evacuated 233 students and civilians back to Point Salines. Once all of the students were airborne, the Sea Knights returned to pick up the Rangers as they disengaged from their positions around the campus in phases. In the hurried departure, 11 Rangers were

One of the CH-46 Sea Knight helicopters carrying Rangers to Grand Anse had to be left behind after it struck a palm tree along the narrow beach during the student rescue mission. The more extensive damage to the nose was inflicted later from the fire of a Spectre gunship ordered to destroy sensitive equipment onboard. (National Archives)

RANGERS RESCUE THE STUDENTS AT GRAND ANSE, 1630HRS, OCTOBER 26, 1983 (PP.76–77)

A main objective of the second day of Operation *Urgent Fury* was to rescue the US medical students from the second campus of St George's Medical School located at Grand Anse. US forces had been shocked to learn on the first morning of the campaign that the medical school's main campus, along with more than two-thirds of its students, was located at Grand Anse rather than True Blue and remained well behind enemy lines.

Seeking a rapid way to reach the students at Grand Anse on October 26, Maj. Gen. Norman Schwarzkopf and Vice Adm. Joseph Metcalf, aboard the flagship USS *Guam* offshore (1), devised a plan for Rangers at Point Salines to fly on Marine helicopters directly to Grand Anse Beach to evacuate the students from the seaward direction. After an artillery and air bombardment of suspected Grenadian positions in the area, nine CH-46 Sea Knights in waves of three deployed 150 Rangers from the 2nd Battalion, but one helicopter became disabled when its rotors tangled with a palm tree lining the narrow beach (2). While Lt Col. Ralph Hagler of the

Rangers and Lt Col. Granville Amos of HMM-261 circled in their command helicopter offshore (3), five CH-53 Sea Stallions landed successively on the beach to ferry the students to safety (4). The Rangers maintained defensive positions around the campus and landing zone (5) while others guided the students from a dormitory building across the beach and into the helicopters waiting in the surf (6).

The Rangers evacuated all 233 students and civilians unharmed to Point Salines, marking a high point of the campaign for US forces. The damaged Sea Knight was able to take off and return to Point Salines as well, though a second met a similar fate on its return to pick up the Rangers when its rotors became entangled with a palm tree along the shoreline, causing more severe damage that forced its abandonment. In the rushed evacuation, 11 Rangers were left behind and had to escape in life rafts to Navy ships offshore.

accidentally left behind. Improvising their escape, these Rangers used life rafts from the disabled helicopter left on the beach to row out to Navy ships offshore rather than risk traveling overland back to the lines of the 82nd Airborne.

The rescue of the medical students from Grand Anse marked a high point of the operation and a fitting coda for the Rangers who had stood at the center of the fighting since it had first broken out the previous morning. Though five Rangers were wounded from the light resistance of Grenadian forces, none had been killed and all the students were safe. The mission, which had lasted only 26 minutes, showcased the abilities of the American commanders – from Metcalf and Schwarzkopf down to Hagler and Amos – to improvise a complex joint-service mission on short notice. The only development to mar the otherwise successful mission was the unwelcome news that several hundred more medical students still lay outside the reach of American protection, mainly in private residences on the Lance aux Épines peninsula east of Point Salines.

For the time being, however, the Rangers and students felt justified in celebrating. As the relieved students enthusiastically welcomed the Rangers on their return to the Point Salines airstrip, one Ranger pumped his fist and assured them, "We do embassies too!" At about the same time, at 1719hrs, another iconic moment was unfolding at Charleston Air Force Base, where the first group of American medical students rescued from Grenada landed back in the US. One of the first students off the plane dropped to his knees on the runway and kissed the ground in relief and celebration.

DAY 3: SELF-INFLICTED WOUNDS

By the end of the second day of combat, the battle for control of Grenada was all but over. However, plagued by repeated and alarming (but erroneous) reports of large forces of Cuban and Grenadian troops still stationed around

When the first flight of American students evacuated from Grenada landed on American soil on the evening of October 26, one of the students fell to his knees and kissed the ground – an iconic moment that helped swing American public opinion decisively in support of the military operation. (National Archives)

Day 3 of Operation *Urgent Fury*, October 27, 1983

Calivigny Military Compound

②

Fort Frederick

Richmond Hill Prison

①

22 MAU — Faulkner/ Smith

Mount Wheldale (Government House)

Queen's Park Racetrack

Fort Rupert

St George's

xx TG 20.5 — Berry

③

Lance aux Épines

82 PRA/PRM

Silvasy — x 2 — 82

④

Grand Anse Beach

Grand Anse Medical School Campus

TF 124 — x — Erie

82 Scott — x 3 — 82

Frequente

True Blue Medical School Campus

Calliste

xxx JTF — Metcalf — 120

82 Trobaugh — xx TF 121

75 Hagler — R 2 — 75

C 1/75 Barno — R 1/75

75 Taylor — R 1 — 75

Lewis — CPF

GRAND BAY

Point Salines

1. Marines advance unopposed from the northern and eastern outskirts of St George's to secure the forts surrounding the capital, then move into the city itself, reaching south of the harbor by nightfall.
2. At 1600hrs, the Army, Navy, and Air Force bombard the Calivigny compound with artillery and airpower to precede the Ranger assault.
3. At 1645hrs, the 2nd Ranger Battalion leads a helicopter assault on Calivigny, where a crash-landing results in casualties; the Rangers secure the compound by 2100hrs.
4. At 1645hrs, a Navy Corsair jet accidentally strafes the 82nd Airborne brigade command post as the 2nd Brigade advances north toward St George's.

N

1 mile

1km

0

0

80

the island, American commanders did not yet seem to understand this fact. As the Marines and the 82nd Airborne continued their cautious advance on October 27, the third day of the campaign, the blood that US forces would continue to shed tragically came more from their own mishaps – accidents and friendly fire – than from enemy combat.

Marines move south

One of the main objectives of the third day of *Urgent Fury* was the linkup of the Marines and the 82nd Airborne to the south of the capital city. From its position at Fort Frederick, the Marine battalion of Lt Col. Ray Smith was ordered to continue its advance south to complete the capture of the strongpoints surrounding St George's before moving into the capital itself.

When they arrived at Richmond Hill Prison at 0800hrs, the Marines found this target of the aborted Delta Force mission on October 25 to be abandoned, capturing it with no opposition. The prison guards had fled their posts early on the previous day when the rest of the PRA's organized resistance began to melt away. Several hundred prisoners, a mix of criminals and political detainees, had already escaped by the time the Marines arrived to find only a handful still in their cells.

With all the key forts overlooking the capital now in American hands, the Marines advanced into St George's itself, finding no resistance and an enthusiastic welcome from Grenadian civilians, who assisted in identifying hidden weapons caches and PRA members who had shed their uniforms. By evening, the Marines reached the Ross Point Inn south of St George's Harbour and secured a group of mainly Canadian foreign nationals. They then set up a defensive perimeter around the seaside hotel at 1930hrs to await the arrival of the 82nd Airborne at their rendezvous point.

Crash at Calivigny, friendly fire at Frequente

The Rangers had one final operation to carry out on Grenada, and they considered it a suicide mission. They were proven correct, in that it became one of the bloodiest moments of the campaign for American forces, but not for the reasons they expected. The ill-fated attack on Calivigny proved to be one of the most tragic episodes of the Grenada campaign, an unfortunate finale for the Army Rangers who had borne the brunt of the fighting since the first day of the operation.

Around noon on October 27, Adm. Metcalf received an urgent message from his superiors in the US directing him to launch an immediate assault on the Grenadian military compound near the village of Calivigny, on a remote peninsula about 5 miles to the east of Point Salines. The Calivigny compound, constructed by the Cubans, was the main base and training facility for the PRA regular forces. US intelligence believed that the military camp also served as a Cuban training center for exporting communist revolution throughout the Caribbean region. American military planners assumed that this high-value target would be heavily defended, and the US forces assigned to carry out the attack expected to meet a full battalion of Grenadian soldiers reinforced by 300 or more Cuban troops, a total force of as many as 600 that also wielded six antiaircraft guns. Given the bloody record to date of American daylight helicopter assaults in Grenada, the US soldiers and pilots tasked with the mission prepared to meet stiff resistance.

Metcalf passed the urgent orders on to Gen. Trobaugh, who assigned the mission to the Rangers' 2nd Battalion, which had carried out the successful rescue of medical students at Grand Anse the day before. Now relieved of their duties around Point Salines Airport, the Rangers had been preparing to fly back to their base in the US. Instead, a force of about 180, under the command of Lt Col. Hagler and the newly arrived commander of the 82nd Airborne's 3rd Brigade, Col. James Scott, would mount a helicopter assault on the compound in four successive waves of four Black Hawks each.

The attack began at 1600hrs with the largest artillery bombardment of the campaign. With little chance of collateral damage near the isolated compound, situated on a plateau with steep cliffs leading down to the sea, Metcalf unleashed the full weight of his arsenal: Army artillery from Point Salines, Navy surface guns and Corsair jets, and an Air Force Spectre gunship all trained their sights on reducing the barracks and training buildings in the Calivigny compound to rubble before the Rangers arrived. Hagler and Scott, watching the bombardment from their command helicopter, were dismayed to see the Army artillery rounds drop harmlessly into the sea short of their target, while the Navy vessels hardly fired any rounds at all. The aerial bombardment from Navy jets and an Air Force gunship proved far more effective, blasting the buildings and setting them ablaze.

As smoke billowed from the Calivigny compound and obscured their view of what they would face, the Rangers began their assault at 1645hrs. The first wave of four Black Hawk helicopters approached the peninsula

A massive artillery bombardment preceded the ill-fated Ranger attack on the PRA's Calivigny compound. Though it was the Grenadian military's main base and training facility, the compound was virtually deserted by the time the Rangers launched their attack. (National Archives)

at low altitude and high speed, quickly climbing up the steep cliffs to find their landing zone inside the compound on the plateau above. The first two helicopters landed smoothly, but the third Black Hawk's tail suffered damage while it was still in the air, causing it to crash-land into the second. The damage may have come from small-arms fire from the small squad of Grenadian soldiers spotted nearby or from exploding ammunition stores within one of the burning buildings in the compound – exacerbated by the helicopters' difficult approach that caused them to come in too fast and overshoot their landing zone. The fourth Black Hawk veered to avoid the tangled helicopters and crash-landed in a ditch, suffering damage of its own that turned catastrophic when the pilot tried to take off and instead spun out of control, colliding with the other two and sending severed rotors flying in all directions. The crash killed three Rangers and gravely wounded numerous others.

The remaining waves of Rangers, assuming that the wrecked helicopters had been shot down, braced for carnage of their own. But the rest of Hagler's Ranger force landed successfully to find the compound completely deserted. The few Grenadian defenders who had been stationed there had fled at the start of the artillery bombardment an hour before. As Gen. Schwarzkopf later lamented, Calivigny turned out to be a "dry hole" where "we'd been chasing ghosts." The Rangers secured the compound by 2100hrs and spent the night among the rubble.

While the attack on Calivigny was unfolding, a friendly fire incident inflicted a heavy toll on the 82nd Airborne advancing north and east from the Point Salines airfield. Several units of paratroopers came under

The Ranger assault on Calivigny occurred in four waves of four Black Hawks each. The first two helicopters landed successfully, but the next two crashed, with disastrous results. The follow-on waves of Rangers feared that the Black Hawks had been shot down and prepared for the worst, but they found the compound deserted. (National Archives)

Grenadian sniper fire near a crossroads to the east of Frequente and called in air support from Navy jets to silence the threat at 1645hrs. Miscommunication between the soldiers on the ground and the pilots in the air led a Corsair jet to mistakenly strafe the command post of Col. Stephen Silvasy's 2nd Brigade of the 82nd Airborne on a ridge near Frequente rather than the source of the sniper fire nearby. Silvasy was unharmed, but the Corsair attack blew the roof off the command post building and left 17 members of the brigade staff wounded, including one paratrooper with a mortal wound.

FINAL PHASE AND END OF HOSTILITIES

After the third day of combat, the reality of the collapse of substantial resistance from Grenadian and Cuban forces began to sink in for American commanders. With the island's strategic points all under the control of the US–Caribbean coalition, the focus of the remainder of the campaign shifted from combat to mopping-up operations. The Marines in the north and the 82nd Airborne in the south extended their control to the more remote regions of Grenada, continuing their search for hidden stores of weapons and the fugitive leaders of the toppled RMC regime.

The most important and urgent task for US forces was to locate and secure the remaining American medical students scattered around Grenada. Finally, at 0730hrs on October 28, 82nd Airborne paratroopers advancing north from Point Salines linked up with the Marines at the Ross Point Inn, just

American students from St George's University Medical School celebrate their rescue from the Grand Anse campus on October 26. By the end of the campaign, US forces evacuated a total of 581 American citizens. (National Archives)

south of St George's, consolidating their hold on the most populous region of the island. Shortly afterwards, at 0814hrs, another group of paratroopers secured an additional 202 American students and other civilians living off-campus in private residences on the Lance aux Épines peninsula. By the end of the morning, the final group of American students and civilians scattered around the island had been evacuated to Point Salines, bringing the total number of American students rescued to 581.

Thanks to intelligence provided by Grenadian civilians, US forces were able to round up the leaders of the Grenadian regime over the next few days. Gen. Hudson Austin, the chairman of the RMC and commander of the PRA, and Bernard Coard, the leader of the coup against Bishop and unofficial chief of the RMC, had been on the run and in hiding since fleeing from their Fort Frederick command post in the early-morning hours of October 26. They sought in vain a means of escaping from the island to seek refuge in Guyana or another sympathetic country, knowing that the Cubans would offer no sanctuary. With the island tightly blockaded by the US Navy, the fugitives found shelter where they could. Acting on a tip from local civilians, Marines captured Coard and several followers in a private residence on the eastern outskirts of St George's on the morning of October 29. The following afternoon, 82nd Airborne paratroopers captured Austin, along with his deputy, Lt Col. Ewart Layne, in a private home at Westerhall Point on the island's southern coast. These deposed leaders were initially detained aboard USS *Guam* before taking up more permanent residence in Richmond Hill Prison, where they awaited trial for the murder of Bishop and his supporters on Bloody Wednesday.

Gen. John Vessey (center right) tours American military positions on Grenada on October 30. Hoping to prevent an insurgency, he urged Maj. Gen. Edward Trobaugh (center left) to secure the rest of the island and bring hostilities to a rapid close. (National Archives)

Though US commanders in Grenada realized that the end of the campaign was near, fears lingered in the Pentagon that large numbers of Cuban combatants had escaped into the mountainous interior of Grenada to wage a guerilla campaign. Gen. John Vessey, the chairman of the Joint Chiefs of Staff, and Adm. Wesley McDonald, the commander in chief of Atlantic Command, visited Grenada on October 30 to inspect the progress of the campaign, urging the on-scene commanders to quickly secure the rest of the Grenadian mainland. Before the day was out, the Marines secured the three major towns along Grenada's northern coast. Two days later, on November 1, in the last significant combat operation of the campaign, the Marines made a helicopter and amphibious landing on Carriacou, Grenada's second-largest island to the north, encountering no resistance as they secured the last potential bastion for renegade Grenadians or Cubans.

US and coalition forces declared an official end of hostilities at 1500hrs on November 2, eight days after the invasion began. That same day, the Marines departed the island en route to their delayed peacekeeping duties in Lebanon, and Adm. Metcalf turned over command of US forces in Grenada to Gen. Trobaugh, whose 82nd Airborne paratroopers soon began their own withdrawal as they handed over longer-term peacekeeping duties to the Caribbean Peacekeeping Force. The last American combat soldiers departed Grenada on December 12. They left in their wake a war-torn island transitioning back to the camp of democratic nations – a moral victory for the forces of anticommunism that marked the beginning of the end of the Cold War.

The last contingent of American soldiers stands at attention as the US flag is lowered for the final time at Point Salines Airport, marking the formal end of the US military presence on Grenada. (Mike Leahy, Navy Art Collection, Naval History and Heritage Command)

AFTERMATH

"It is in Grenada that the fall of communism began," declared Sir Paul Scoon after the American-led military campaign restored democracy to the island nation in the fall of 1983. Scoon was correct that the invasion of Grenada marked a watershed moment in the final decade of the Cold War. This small-scale campaign had a disproportionately large and far-reaching legacy that reshaped the trajectory of global affairs. Its impact on Grenada and the United States lasted long after the guns fell silent – and even beyond the end of the Cold War.

As the dust of battle settled, the human toll of the campaign came into clearer view. US military forces suffered 19 killed – eight Army Rangers, four Navy SEALs, three 82nd Airborne paratroopers, three Marine pilots, and one special forces pilot. Of these, ten were killed by enemy fire, while the other nine died from combat-related accidents. The estimated total of American wounded, including the official tally and additional unacknowledged wounded from special operations missions, came to 157. Cuban forces, including construction workers and military advisors, suffered 25 killed and 59 wounded. The Cuban prisoners and dead were repatriated to their homeland in early November 1983. The fighting took its highest toll on Grenadian forces, with 45 PRA soldiers and PRM militiamen killed and 358 Grenadians wounded (including combatants and civilians). At least 24 Grenadian civilians also died during the battle, including 21 patients killed in the accidental bombing of the mental hospital. This higher death toll on Grenadian combatants underscores the fact – little understood in the US government and military at the time and since – that the main enemy that faced US forces and put up the stoutest resistance in the campaign was the Grenadians, not the Cubans.

The period of upheaval on Grenada between the coup against Maurice Bishop and the defeat of the new regime at the hands of the US–Caribbean coalition in October 1983 had brought the island nation to the brink of civil war. The military campaign removed the violent and repressive RMC, but it left the country bruised and battered. Most critical and urgent for the future of Grenada was the need to rebuild a national government and restore democratic institutions. Governor-General Scoon moved quickly and decisively to assume the reins of restructuring the Grenadian government, taking executive action as the only remaining legitimate governing authority left in the wake of the island's political tumult. Scoon's first order of business was to restore the democratic constitution that Bishop had suspended

President Reagan, alongside First Lady Nancy Reagan, attends a ceremony on November 4, 1983 to honor the fallen and wounded from the fighting in Grenada as well as the terrorist attack in Lebanon. These twin crises marked one of the most challenging periods of Reagan's presidency. (Courtesy Ronald Reagan Presidential Library)

following his seizure of power in 1979. After severing diplomatic relations with the Soviet Union and other communist countries (though not with neighboring Cuba) and expelling the Cuban ambassador, Scoon appointed an Advisory Council on November 15, 1983, to serve as the interim government and organize new elections on Grenada. These democratic elections – the first on Grenada since 1976 – were held on December 3, 1984, resulting in the election of Herbert Blaize as prime minister at the helm of a center–right coalition. Grenada remains a democracy to the present day.

The violent demise of Bishop's government looms in Grenadian collective memory as a more resonant and painful episode than the military invasion itself. After a lengthy trial, Bernard Coard, Hudson Austin, and 12 other members of the RMC and PRA were convicted in Grenadian criminal court in December 1986 of murdering Bishop and seven of his supporters on Bloody Wednesday. Though sentenced to hang, their death sentences were commuted to life in prison in 1991, and the last prisoners (including Coard) were released in 2009. The vast majority of the Grenadian people greeted the American-led invasion with what Scoon called "overwhelming support" and a sense of liberation. Each year, Grenadians celebrate October 25, the anniversary of the start of the invasion, as Thanksgiving Day, a public holiday.

The safe return of the American medical students ensured widespread public support in the United States for the Reagan administration's decision to launch the military intervention on Grenada. The successful operation contributed to the political boost that resulted in President Reagan's reelection in November 1984 in one of the biggest landslide victories in American history. Reagan himself was exceptionally pleased with the US military's performance in Grenada, calling the operation "a textbook

12TH ANNIVERSARY OF THE LIBERATION OF GRENADA

U.S. PRESIDENT RONALD W. REAGAN
LEADER OF THE COMBINED FORCES OF LIBERATION

Though controversial abroad, the US-led military campaign found widespread popular support in the United States and Grenada. Grenadians have commemorated their "liberation" with memorabilia including these stamps featuring St George's Harbour behind the likeness of Ronald Reagan, "Leader of the Combined Forces of Liberation." (Author's Collection)

success" that was "planned beautifully & executed even better." But others, including Norman Schwarzkopf and Colin Powell – then serving as a major general on the staff of the secretary of defense – formed a more critical assessment of Operation *Urgent Fury*. Powell later called the Grenada campaign "a sloppy success" due to its poor cooperation and communication between the military services, as well as intelligence failures and problems with a convoluted chain of command. "I filed away the lessons learned," he noted, and so too did the US government, even while it celebrated Grenada as a success. The flaws of *Urgent Fury* prompted Congress to pass the Goldwater–Nichols Act, which Reagan signed into law in October 1986, reforming the Defense Department and the command structure of the US military by incorporating the lessons of the Grenada operation. Powell and Schwarzkopf benefited from these reforms when they later worked together during the Gulf War in 1990–91.

The Grenada campaign contributed to turning the tide of the Cold War and hastening its end on terms favorable to the US and its allies. Though its immediate military benefits were limited and remote from the Cold War's key flashpoints in Europe and Asia, the invasion of Grenada demonstrated a reinvigoration of the US military's capabilities after the setback of Vietnam – and a reinvigoration of the resolve of the American people and their leaders to reverse communist expansion. The military success gave the American public a morale boost that helped it overcome the hesitancy to use military force abroad that had become known as the "Vietnam syndrome." Secretary of State George Shultz called Grenada "a shot heard round the world" with "a strong rippling effect in faraway places," demonstrating to the Soviet Union and its communist allies that Reagan was prepared to back his strong anticommunist rhetoric with action.

In the short term, the international community, including longstanding US allies such as Britain, widely condemned the American military intervention on Grenada, and the campaign contributed to the heightening of Cold War tensions in the fall of 1983. But the clear demonstration of American capabilities and resolve soon helped to recalibrate relations between the US and the Soviet Union toward diplomacy and negotiations that led to a landmark treaty to reduce both countries' nuclear arsenals. Before the end of the decade, what Scoon called "the gale force wind of change" that started on Grenada swept across Eastern Europe and eventually the Soviet Union itself as the Berlin Wall fell and communist regimes were replaced by democracies.

For all its importance to the end of the Cold War, Grenada's most enduring legacy came in moving the American military toward the post-Cold War world. The reforms that Operation *Urgent Fury* inspired and the leaders that the campaign shaped created the military force that would face new threats in the era to come, from "rogue states" such as Iraq to terrorist networks after 9/11. The Grenada invasion, a small but complex contingency operation aimed at regime change, set new precedents for the use of American military force that would outlast the Cold War and shape the conflicts of the coming years, from the invasion of Panama and the Gulf War to the War on Terror.

On February 20, 1986, Air Force One touched down on the now-completed runway of Point Salines International Airport in Grenada. President Reagan toured key sites of the battle and unveiled a memorial to the Americans who served and died in the military campaign. Then he met with Grenadian and Caribbean leaders, including Sir Paul Scoon and Eugenia Charles, in the same dining room in Government House where Scoon had taken shelter with Navy SEALs. Finally, the President made his way to the former Marine command post at Queen's Park near St George's to deliver a speech before an estimated 42,000 Grenadians. Reagan greeted his listeners as "friends who share a fundamental belief in democracy" and assured them that there was "a freedom tide rising in our hemisphere." The Grenada campaign marked a resurgence of American resolve to harness this rising tide to end the Cold War and shape the new world order beyond.

President Reagan speaks to a huge crowd at the Queen's Park Racetrack during his visit to Grenada in 1986. Colin Powell, who accompanied Reagan on the trip, noted that he had "never witnessed an outburst of mass emotion to match the President's welcome in Grenada." (Courtesy Ronald Reagan Presidential Library)

THE BATTLEFIELD TODAY

Though many of Grenada's key battlefield sites today lie in ruins, the scars of the battle for Grenada remain plainly visible as stark reminders of the military conflict that engulfed the island nation over four decades ago.

The airport at Point Salines was completed with American aid and opened in 1984, renamed Maurice Bishop International Airport in 2009 for the prime minister whose death triggered the military campaign. It is now Grenada's only functioning airport and is the point of entry for visitors from around the world. A memorial to the US and Caribbean forces, "especially those who sacrificed their lives in liberating Grenada," stands in a small park next to the airport terminal.

St George's University expanded dramatically from the early 1990s, transforming its satellite campus at True Blue from a handful of modest

President Reagan dedicates a memorial to the 19 US servicemen killed in Operation *Urgent Fury* during his visit to Grenada on February 20, 1986. Originally located at the Grand Anse campus of St George's University, it has since been relocated to True Blue, now the medical school's main campus. (Courtesy Ronald Reagan Presidential Library)

structures to a vast footprint of over 60 buildings that resembles a resort. The former main campus at Grand Anse was closed and is no longer in operation, though the buildings remain. Meanwhile, Grand Anse Beach is now widely considered one of the most picturesque beaches in the Caribbean and hosts numerous tourist resorts.

The main sites around St George's are currently in varied stages of disrepair and restoration. Government House was severely damaged by a hurricane in 2004, and was subsequently abandoned and fell into ruin. Efforts to raise funds to restore the building are ongoing but have not yet borne fruit. Fort Frederick is the best-preserved fort on Grenada and is open to the public, providing a window into the island's colonial past. Fort Rupert's name was restored to Fort George soon after the military campaign. Recently renovated, it is open to the public and offers panoramic views of St George's Harbour. A plaque in the courtyard marks the place where Maurice Bishop was executed on Bloody Wednesday. Richmond Hill Prison remains in operation.

Further afield, the Calivigny military compound was abandoned in the aftermath of the campaign, and the Egmont peninsula on which it was built has since been developed into a residential area. The Radio Free Grenada station building is still standing near Beauséjour north of St George's, but is not operational and the transmitter has been removed.

On Grenada's northeast coast, Pearls Airport closed in 1984 but is still standing, unused. The overgrown wrecks of two aircraft, a Cubana Airlines turboprop and a Soviet biplane, sit near the former terminal, ghostly relics of the 1983 battle for Grenada.

Two planes captured by American forces still lie near the former terminal building at Pearls Airport, including this Cubana Airlines turboprop that landed the day before the invasion began, carrying Col. Pedro Tortoló Comas to take command of Cuban forces on Grenada. The planes now sit in ruins. (Robert Nickelsberg/Getty Images)

BIBLIOGRAPHY AND FURTHER READING

Author's note: The works listed below were the sources most central to the research for this book. The three most useful books for studying the military history of the Grenada campaign are Mark Adkin's *Urgent Fury* (1989), Edgar Raines's *The Rucksack War* (2010), and Philip Kukielski's *The U.S. Invasion of Grenada* (2019). Adkin's *Urgent Fury* stood for many years as the most detailed and engaging narrative account of the operation. While less reliable on the specifics of US military action, it remains valuable for its knowledgeable coverage of the Grenadian and Caribbean perspectives. Raines's *Rucksack War* more recently claimed the mantle as the most comprehensively researched study of each phase of the operation, with a particular focus on logistics and the US Army's role. However, its sheer density makes it more of a reference work than an engaging narrative history. Kukielski's *U.S. Invasion of Grenada* balances thorough, up-to-date research with a well-rounded but concise narrative that incorporates the political, diplomatic, and military dimensions of the campaign. It is therefore this author's recommendation for the next stop for the interested reader.

Adkin, Mark, *Urgent Fury: The Battle for Grenada*, Lexington Books, Lexington, MA (1989)

Badri-Maharaj, Sanjay, *Urgent Fury: Grenada 1983*, Helion, Warwick, UK (2022)

Bennett, Ralph Kinney, "Grenada: Anatomy of a 'Go' Decision," in *Reader's Digest* 124, no. 742 (February 1984), pp. 72–77

Burrowes, Reynold A., *Revolution and Rescue in Grenada: An Account of the U.S.–Caribbean Invasion*, Greenwood Press, New York (1988)

Cannon, Lou, *President Reagan: The Role of a Lifetime*, revised edition, PublicAffairs, New York (2000)

Chalker, Dennis, with Dockery, Kevin, *One Perfect Op: An Insider's Account of the Navy SEAL Special Warfare Teams*, William Morrow, New York (2002)

Cole, Ronald H., *Operation Urgent Fury: The Planning and Execution of Joint Operations in Grenada, 12 October–2 November 1983*, Joint History Office, Office of the Chairman of the Joint Chiefs of Staff, Washington, DC (1997)

Crandall, Russell, *Gunboat Democracy: U.S. Interventions in the Dominican Republic, Grenada, and Panama*, Rowman and Littlefield, Lanham, MD (2006)

Gormly, Robert A., *Combat Swimmer: Memoirs of a Navy SEAL*, Dutton, New York (1998)

Greer, Tom, and Muccia, Joe, *Cry Havoc! An Untold Story of Rangers at War*, Military History Research and Publishing, Fredericksburg, VA (2023)

Huchthausen, Peter, *America's Splendid Little Wars: A Short History of U.S. Engagements: From the Fall of Saigon to Baghdad*, Penguin Books, New York (2003)

Inboden, William, *The Peacemaker: Ronald Reagan, the Cold War, and the World on the Brink*, Dutton, New York (2022)

Kukielski, Philip, *The U.S. Invasion of Grenada: Legacy of a Flawed Victory*, McFarland, Jefferson, NC (2019)

McFarlane, Robert C., with Smardz, Zofia, *Special Trust*, Cadell and Davies, New York (1994)

Metcalf, Joseph, III, "Decision Making and the Grenada Rescue Operation," in *Ambiguity and Command: Organizational Perspectives on Military Decision Making*, edited by James G. March and Roger Weissinger-Baylon, Pitman, Marshfield, MA (1986), pp. 277–97

Moore, Charles, *Margaret Thatcher: The Authorized Biography*, vol. 2, *Everything She Wants*, Penguin Books, London (2015)

O'Shaughnessy, Hugh, *Grenada: Revolution, Invasion, and Aftermath*, Sphere Books, London (1984)

Payne, Anthony, Sutton, Paul, and Thorndike, Tony, *Grenada: Revolution and Invasion*, Croom Helm, London (1984)

Raines, Edgar F., Jr., *Operation Urgent Fury: The Invasion of Grenada, October 1983*, edited by Richard W. Stewart, US Army Center of Military History, Washington, DC (2008)

Raines, Edgar F., Jr., *The Rucksack War: U.S. Army Operational Logistics in Grenada, 1983*, US Army Center of Military History, Washington, DC (2010)

Reagan, Ronald, *An American Life*, Simon & Schuster, New York (1990)

Reagan, Ronald, *The Reagan Diaries*, edited by Douglas Brinkley, HarperCollins, New York (2007)

Russell, Lee E., and Mendez, M. Albert, *Grenada 1983*, Osprey, London (1985)

Schwarzkopf, H. Norman, with Petre, Peter, *It Doesn't Take a Hero*, Linda Grey Bantam Books, New York (1992)

Scoon, Paul, *Survival for Service: My Experiences as Governor General of Grenada*, Macmillan Caribbean, Oxford (2003)

Shultz, George P., *Turmoil and Triumph: My Years as Secretary of State*, Charles Scribner's Sons, New York (1993)

Spector, Ronald H., *U.S. Marines in Grenada, 1983*, US Marine Corps History and Museums Division, Washington, DC (1987)

Weinberger, Caspar W., *Fighting for Peace: Seven Critical Years in the Pentagon*, Warner Books, New York (1990)

Williams, Gary, *US–Grenada Relations: Revolution and Intervention in the Backyard*, Palgrave Macmillan, New York (2007)

INDEX

Figures in **bold** refer to illustrations.